The Magic of Rapport

The Magic
of
Rapport

How You Can Gain
Personal Power
in Any Situation

Jerry Richardson

META PUBLICATIONS
P.O. Box 1910
Capitola, CA 95010
(831) 464-0254
FAX (831) 464-0517
www.meta-publications.com

Library of Congress Card Number 00-133253
ISBN 0-916990-44-3

Dedication

To the memory of my father, Hervey Stafford "Tat" Richardson, who taught me much of what I know about interpersonal communication, certainly much more than either he or I was aware of, and to whom I will be forever beholden.

Acknowledgements

I would like to acknowledge some of the people who've made this book and this second edition possible:

Richard Bandler, who spent a lot of time with me during the 1970s when I was initially exposed to NLP, for sharing with me his insights—invariably brilliant, often outlandish, usually provocative, and always stimulating—into this most interesting filter for understanding human behavior. Richard was always generous with his time and ideas and I will always be grateful for his influence and guidance.

Lynn Lannon, my wife and partner and best friend, who continues to inspire me with her love and deep insights into the nature of communication and from whom I've learned much about what it takes to make a relationship work—personally, professionally, and spiritually. For her great help and support in revising this book and for her tireless attempts to get me to practice what I preach.

The thousands of individuals in the many organizations with whom I've consulted over the years, for helping me clarify both my thinking and my presentation of the material.

My many friends and colleagues who have shared with me their stories about how the ideas in this book have helped them be even more effective in their dealings with others.

Joel Margulis, my co-author of the first edition, for his insights and many stories and examples that continue to enrich the text.

The body of NLP practitioners, writers, speakers, trainers and others who have made their techniques and strategies available to me and the rest of the community of readers who are deeply interested in the practical applications of this technology.

Jenny D'Angelo, whose capable edit of the manuscript of this second edition helped unify its sometimes disparate tones.

And last, but certainly not least, my mother, Madelyn Richardson, who has always been my loyal supporter and an inspiration to find the high ground in both thinking and in communication.

San Francisco, California   Jerry Richardson
May 2000

Contents

Preface to the Second Edition

The world has changed a lot since the first edition of *The Magic of Rapport* was published. Perhaps of the most important changes have been the evolution of electronic communication and the development of the Internet. However, even though the context has changed, the principles of communication have not. Interpersonal communication does not seem to be subject to the same life cycles as technological products, which get shorter and shorter.

Interpersonal communication is different. What was true twenty years ago is true today, will most likely to be true in another twenty or, perhaps, even two hundred years. Human beings don't seem to change that much, although some would argue that on Internet time we've become more short-sighted in our goal-setting and less patient with each other.

In addition to electronic communication and commerce, a corresponding development has been the downsizing of our organizations. Some would say the appropriate word is "right-sizing." Whatever word is used, it's apparent that employees are now expected to do more with less. One of the most common changes in the organizations I've worked with recently is that the environment has become one of increasing demands and diminishing resources. Organizations have frequently become more profitable, but the working conditions have often become less hospitable. In this high-demand, low-resource work world, communication has to produce more results in less time.

This change argues the need for even better communication skills. Good communication skills will generally shorten the amount of time it takes to get things done through people. There will be fewer breakdowns in communication and more efficient exchanges of ideas when everyone has better interpersonal skills.

In fact, good interpersonal skills are a critical success factor in all aspects of life. Since the publication of *The Magic of Rapport* one of the most interesting investigations in the area of interpersonal communication has come from psychologist Daniel Goleman and his development of the concept "Emotional Intelligence." Emotional Intelligence—or emotional literacy, the term he prefers—has to do with the importance of self-management and interpersonal skills in determining both personal and professional success. Goleman's work cites numerous studies that support a major thesis of this book; namely, that the critical success factors in life have more to do with how you deal with yourself and with others than with cognitive or intellectual abilities. This is not to say that cognitive ability isn't important, merely that it is not as important as you may have been led to believe. This will come as no surprise to anyone familiar with the "good student" syndrome, i.e., one can be a good student in school but a failure in life. The two situations require different skill sets. *Emotional Intelligence* and *The Magic of Rapport* both address the importance of interpersonal skills over cognitive ability as the determining factor in both personal and professional success. In *Emotional Intelligence*, Goleman also addresses the importance of *intra*-personal skills. In the first edition of *The Magic of Rapport* I approached success primarily from the standpoint of inter-personal skills; in this edition I've added a section on "Rapport with the Self," which deals with some of the same intra-personal issues that Goleman addresses.

A note on the sub-title of this book, "How to Gain Personal Power in Any Situation": I define personal power as the ability to get other people to do things because they want to, not because they have to. I distinguish personal power from positional power, in which your ability to influence other people derives from authority, from your position in the organizational hierarchy or your ability to give or withdraw rewards. When you have *personal* power, you are able to influence people to do things because they want to do them. When you have *positional* power you are able to influence people to do things because they have to do them. You can think of this as a series of steps, as follows:

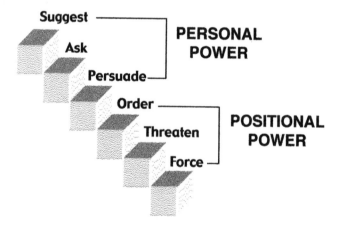

An important thing to keep in mind is that, having once started the descent, it's much easier to go down the steps than it is to come back up. If my *suggestion* doesn't work, it's a simple enough thing to *ask* you to do something. If that doesn't work I can proceed to attempts at *persuasion*. However, once I've issued an *order* (assuming I have the authority to do so), if I fail to get compliance it's unlikely that I'm going to try persuasion or more asking. It's more likely that I'm going to *threaten* you with dire consequences if you don't comply. If you still don't comply I may have to resort to some form of *force*. Generally this doesn't involve the use of physical force, although there is always lurking behind this option the authority to use physical force or to get others to use it. For example, if I'm your boss I have the authority to order you to do something. If you don't comply with my order I can threaten you with dire consequences, such as the loss of your job. And if you still don't comply I have the authority to fire you, which might involve calling in the police to forcefully remove you from the premises.

In my experience, the use of positional power, even if you have it, is less preferable than the use of personal power. It's better to get people's willing cooperation than their forced compliance. And that's where the magic of rapport comes in—establishing personal power in any situation.

About the Author

Jerry Richardson is an interpersonal communications consultant with a broad background in training, executive coaching, organizational development, marketing and management consulting, advertising, counseling, and education. He has developed a variety of training, coaching and team-building programs for a wide range of audiences, including both management and non-management, with a special emphasis on the influence process.

Jerry has developed programs for a wide variety of functions including sales, management, customer service, telephone operations, training, and human resources. He has also developed industry-specific programs for various job functions within service and manufacturing organizations. One of his special interests is coaching managers and executives on ways to improve both their own performance and that of their direct reports.

Jerry is a native of Delray Beach, Florida, and is a 1964 graduate of Princeton University, where he majored in English. He has done graduate work in Business and Psychology at Columbia and San Francisco State Universities. Jerry currently heads his own consulting firm, Richardson Associates, which is based in San Francisco. He can be reached at: 800-560-2672; or email him at jerry@richardson.com; or visit the web site at www.richardson.com.

Introduction

This book is designed to help you to be more successful in your dealings with both the people you work with and the people you live with. It's a book for anyone whose professional success or personal satisfaction depends on his or her ability to influence other people. I'll present techniques and strategies that will help you get what you want—whether it be from a client, a boss, a friend, or a spouse.

Reading this book and mastering the techniques and strategies discussed in it will help you to:

- Take control of any situation immediately
- Establish trust and credibility
- Use the power of suggestion to get what you want
- Present your ideas in ways that are virtually irresistible
- Overcome resistance effortlessly and effectively
- Get people to agree with you
- Get other people to clearly understand you
- Avoid being manipulated

Let's look at each of these:

Take control of any situation immediately. Either you control the situation or it controls you. For example, how can you take charge of a group of people who are confused and perhaps threatening? In such situations, many people become paralyzed with fear: The only sure way to take control of this or any situation immediately is (1) determine the prevailing reality of the situation and (2) get into agreement or alignment with that reality. During the course of reading this book, you will learn specific tactics and strategies that you can use to take control and turn the situation in the direction you want it to go.

Establish trust and credibility. During the past few years, many exciting discoveries have come out of research and practice in the social and behavioral sciences. There is more information about why one person likes another, why one person says Yes rather than No to a suggestion, how to deal effectively with change and with resistance to change, how to cope with other people's anger and hostility, and how to clearly communicate ideas to other people so they understand exactly what is being said. *The Magic of Rapport* discusses many of these discoveries in ways that are easy to understand and simple to apply.

Use the power of suggestion to get what you want. Some people have very little trouble getting others to go along with their ideas and suggestions. You too can learn to get exactly what you want whenever you want it.

Present your ideas in ways that are virtually irresistible. When you know more about how other people make decisions than they themselves know, you are in a very powerful position to present your ideas in ways that are almost impossible to resist.

Overcome resistance effortlessly and effectively. When you know how, overcoming other people's resistance is child's play, whether the form of the resistance is an objection to your good idea or a verbal assault on you personally.

Get people to agree with you. You can learn how to establish a pattern of agreement, both verbally and non-verbally, so that others will feel impelled to agree with you.

Get other people to clearly understand you. The secret here is first to understand how other people understand. Then you'll be able to present your ideas in ways that make perfect sense to them.

Avoid being manipulated. Become aware of your own behavioral patterns—the ones that set you up for other people's influence. This is the best way to avoid being manipulated by others.

A Note on NLP (Neuro-Linguistic Programming)

Although this is not a book about NLP, *per se*, many of the techniques and strategies offered in this book come from the body of work known as NLP. NLP issued from the minds and experience of Richard Bandler and John Grinder, whose partnership in the mid-1970s led to this breakthrough technology in the art of human communication. I say "breakthrough" advisedly and intentionally and with full awareness that it's a "hype" word, and I don't intend it to be hype. When I first came upon NLP, I was developing a sales training program for a client and I was looking for new approaches to the subject. A friend, who knew of my search for new information, steered me to an intriguing book entitled *The Structure of Magic* by Bandler and Grinder. The book, in turn, led me to a workshop on hypnosis they were giving in San Francisco. What I discovered at the workshop was that NLP, which was primarily used in therapy at that time, was certainly the most detailed and behaviorally rich description of the persuasive process that I had ever encountered. In that regard, it was truly a breakthrough.

There are various definitions of what NLP is, most of them attempt to wrap meaning around what has become a very large body of practices designed to produce change in others. The first practitioners were interested primarily in the therapeutic applications of NLP. Indeed, the term "Neuro-Linguistic Programming" seems to have a particular appeal for people interested in therapy. In my experience, the term has less appeal for people in business, and since my primary use of the technology is in business I tend to de-emphasize the name and concentrate instead on the outcomes the technology enables. It's a very powerful technology, properly used, and I am indebted to both Richard Bandler and John Grinder for their personally sharing with me much of what I know about NLP. When people ask me, "What is NLP?" I sometimes try to give a complete answer to the question. Usually I'm unsuccessful, because NLP is to human communication what Hinduism is to religion: It seems to be all-inclusive. If a new technology appears on the horizon there is usually an NLP person around to translate it into the language of NLP, usually enriching the new technology in the process. NLP is an all-inclusive and very pragmatic approach to human communication. It tries to accommodate everything. The best definition I've heard of NLP was given to me many years ago by Richard Bandler: "NLP is the study of subjective experience."

Overview of the Book

Part One, *Rapport: What It Is and How to Get It*, shows you how to establish rapport with other people so you can use the power of suggestion to influence them effectively. It also shows you how to establish and maintain rapport with yourself, an important aspect of personal power.

Part Two, *The Art of Clear Communication*, shows you how to identify how other people make sense of things so you can present your ideas in ways that make sense to them.

Part Three, *The Art of Persuasion*, shows you how to find out how other people make decisions so that you can present your ideas in ways that are virtually irresistible. It also takes up the subject of modeling other people's strategies for excellence.

Part Four, *Dealing with Resistance*, shows you how to effortlessly and effectively overcome other people's resistance. It also offers some ideas to help you prevent or contain other people's resistance, whether it's resistance to an idea or a hostile verbal assault.

The Theory Behind the Book

This book is about communication—how to communicate more effectively with the people around you. It is also about persuasion—how to get those people to respond favorably to you and to your suggestions, and to do what you want them to do.

The material derives from recent advances in the state of the communicative and persuasive arts. Drawing on discoveries in such varied fields as hypnosis, cybernetics, linguistics, psychology, and psychiatry, as well as sales and management communications, *The Magic of Rapport* presents in an easy-to-read and simple-to-apply format some of the most exciting and powerful techniques and strategies available for obtaining the support and cooperation of others.

The word communication has come to mean a transferring, imparting, or sharing of information, ideas, messages, or signals. Originally the word had religious connections, deriving as it does from communion. In its original sense, then, communication had to do with a sharing of a significant experience. Thus, the definition becomes: Communication is a sharing of information or experience between or among individuals. The assumption here is that two or more individuals are in communication to the extent that they are sharing common information or experience. Furthermore, the individuals who share this experience may or may not be consciously aware of the sharing.

Much of this book deals with how people process information and attempt to make sense of the world. We all are inundated daily with information and suggestions. Millions of messages filter in and are digested primarily at the unconscious level. We respond unconsciously, and we also act, for the most part, unconsciously. That is, we act automatically, out of habit. We are patterned in our responses to and interactions with others and with the world of messages. Patterns are regular, unvarying ways of acting, doing, or responding.

We are, in other words, creatures of habit. In order for us to function efficiently, habit is necessary and desirable. But being patterned also has its pitfalls. Because we are not always consciously aware of what we're doing or why, we are not always able to reflect on and evaluate which of our habits, or patterns, are functional and which are dysfunctional—which habits are serving us and which are enslaving us.

A major objective of this book is to help you become aware of the patterns in yourself that make it easier for you to get along with and to influence the people with whom you work and live. By becoming more aware of the patterns that serve you well, you can use them even more systematically and appropriately in your dealings with others. Becoming more aware of unconscious patterns that are not serving you, but to which you are unwittingly subservient, allows you to choose. You are free to change those patterns so they no longer interfere in your relations with others.

Sometimes changing your habits is simple to do, requiring only a slightly greater awareness of something you're inadvertently doing or saying. Sometimes it takes a major effort, a concentration of all your powers to dislodge firmly established patterns. Habits die hard—especially those you've lived with for many years. But you can change. The first step is awareness.

Another, and complementary, objective of this book is to enable you to become more aware of behavior patterns in others. When you understand another person's patterns, especially communication patterns, you can predict what that person will probably do when confronted with a particular situation. For example, when you know a person's pattern, or strategy, for making a certain kind of decision, you will know how to influence his or her decision in the future. You can predict with a high degree of reliability how that person will make a similar decision the next time around. Knowing and using another's unconscious patterns gives you the power of persuasion.

But Isn't This Manipulation?

The answer to this question is both Yes and No. Al Smith, while Governor of New York, was once asked about his view of Prohibition and about his position on alcohol. He replied,

> If by alcohol you mean that which is the defiler of innocence, the corrupter of chastity, the scourge of disease, the ruination of the mind and the cause of unemployment and broken families, then of course I oppose it with every resource of mind and body.
>
> But if by alcohol you mean that spirit of fellowship; that oil of conversation which adds lilt to the lips and music to the mouth; that liquid warmth which gladdens the soul and cheers the heart; that benefit whose tax revenue has contributed countless millions into public treasuries to educate our children, to care for the blind and treat our needy elder citizens—then with all the resources of my mind and body I favor it.

Similarly, if by manipulation you mean the unfair taking advantage of another person by devious and insidious means, the unscrupulous depriving of another human being of something precious or valuable for one's own self-indulgent, inconsiderate purpose, then this is not the book for you.

But if by manipulation you mean the skillful use of the communicative and persuasive arts, the dexterous employment of language and diction, the judicious handling of other people's prejudices and predilections, so that the outcome of your

dealings with others is mutually rewarding and productive—
then please read on. This is manipulation in the very best sense
of the term. To the extent you can become even more effective
in such manipulations, you will live and work even more
productively and harmoniously with others. More seriously,
however, I should add here that the techniques and strategies
covered in this book do in fact lend themselves to the first kind
of manipulation. We are dealing here with tools, and tools can
be used both to build and to destroy, to help and to harm. The
choice is left to you, the reader, with this warning. There is a
kind of reciprocity in life: what we do to others is in some form
revisited upon ourselves. As you sow, so shall you reap. Use
these ideas wisely, in the best interest of those you seek to
influence. By so doing, you will also serve yourself and your
own best interests.

PART ONE

Rapport: What It Is and How to Get It

*One judges everyone else by one's own standard and from
one's own standpoint*
—M. Esther Harding

In this part of the book, you'll learn what rapport is together with a technique for immediately establishing rapport with almost anyone. You'll also become familiar with the law of requisite variety and how it can expand your effectiveness with others. You'll learn how to get just about anyone to like you and to agree with your ideas and suggestions. And you'll explore how to "tune into" other people, to "get on their wavelengths," so that you'll understand intuitively what you must do to influence them.

Rapport: What It Is

In the following discussion of what rapport is and how to establish it, keep in mind that rapport forms a key element in persuasion, the art of obtaining the support and cooperation of other people, the art of getting them to do what you want. The techniques and strategies involved in any successful communication all connect in some essential way to rapport.

Dictionaries variously define rapport as a relationship marked by *harmony, conformity, accord, or affinity.* Rapport therefore signals a relationship exemplified by agreement, by alignment, or by likeness or similarity. To the extent, then, that you are in agreement or alignment—whether verbally or non-verbally, or both—with another person, or bear some likeness to him or her, you are in a state of rapport with that person.

There are two ways to look at other people. You can choose to emphasize the differences between you and them. Or you can choose to emphasize the similarities—the things you have in common. If you emphasize the differences, you will find it hard to establish rapport. But if you emphasize what you have in common, resistance and antagonism will disappear. With practice, it becomes easy to find yourself in other people, to ally yourself with them. When this happens, there is cooperation.

This is an exciting venture as well as a profitable one. There are as many different ways of looking at the world as there are people in the world. Expanding your identification with others is like travel—it broadens your horizons. And, as a nice bonus, you get to choose the direction of your travel and to lead others in the same direction.

The Law of Requisite Variety

From cybernetics comes an idea that is extremely useful in dealing with others: *the law of requisite variety.* Cybernetics has to do with the study of automatic control systems, both in humans and in machines. The law of requisite variety[1] states that in any system (whether of humans or machines), all other things being equal, the individual (human or machine) with the widest range of responses will control the system. In plain terms this means that if you have more variety in your behavior than another person, then you can control your interactions with that person. For example, if your client George has five ways of resisting your good idea and you have enough variety in your behavior to deal effectively with each resistant move he makes, you should be able to control the outcome of your interactions with George. In other words, if you can make one move more than George can, you have requisite variety with respect to George.

Think about your own relationships with people. Are there any that really frustrate you? For example, does your nine-year-old constantly interrupt you to complain of boredom? If you have only one suggestion for a new activity, that may not be enough. A rainy day might drive you both nuts. But if you have many suggestions available, you'll have peace and quiet, and the child will be happy and absorbed. The trick is to expand your range. When your range of behavior is wider than the other person's, you should have enough variety to control and direct the situation.[2]

To achieve this requisite (necessary) variety in your behavior, you basically need two things: awareness and flexibility. You need to have enough *awareness* to know whether your communications are being accepted or rejected by others. If you're communicating successfully, then you don't have to make any adjustments—you just keep doing what you've been doing because it's working.

But if what you're doing isn't working, then you need the *flexibility* to change and do something else. And if that doesn't work, then you need to be able to change to something else again, and so on, until you've found what you have to do to get the other person to respond positively to your idea or suggestion.

When people encounter resistance, their response frequently is to push harder with more of the same approach that wasn't working in the first place. This is a good strategy for making the other person even more resistant. When you have requisite variety, you have other options, other patterns, from which to draw until you find one that works with a given individual.

Also, when you encounter someone you want to influence, there is a tendency to assume that it's necessary somehow to change that person. But in fact, it is virtually impossible to change another person. So any attempt to change someone is doomed to failure. Yet when you are with another person you are, whether you intend it or not, having an influence on that person. The influence may be desirable or undesirable—it may be in the direction you want or in a direction away from what you want. The influence may be slight or it may be strong, but it is there.

The approach to communication—and, specifically, persuasive communication—I take in this book is a systems approach. And systems are dynamic; they change. When you change one part of a system, other parts of the system will change in response, to re-establish equilibrium.

Two or more people together comprise a system. Therefore, when you change one person, the other person (or people) will likely respond to the change: This idea implies that if you want to change another person, a good way to start the process is to make some change in yourself and the other person will respond, usually by making some change in him or herself. The question then becomes "What specific change or changes do you need to make in yourself in order to get the desired change in the other person?" That is what requisite variety is about, and that is what this book is about.

There is no guarantee that you will always be able to deal effectively with everyone you meet. It would be nice to be able to make that claim—and deliver on it—but the truth of the matter is that there are some people you just won't be able to get along with, or persuade, or do whatever it is you want to do with them. Not because there isn't something you might do, but simply because you haven't found the pattern that will work with them. Or perhaps because you've decided that it is not worth the effort. But by becoming more flexible in your approaches to others, by becoming more aware of both your own patterns and those of the people you must deal with, you can greatly increase your personal success and satisfaction in the very interesting process of influencing others.

Requisite variety—having enough range in your own behavior to match and even exceed the other person's range—is the foundation on which rapport is built. And building rapport is the best way to overcome others' resistance to what you want them to do.

The Secret of Rapport: Pacing

One of the most powerful strategies for establishing rapport comes to us from Milton Erickson. Before his death in 1979, Erickson was recognized as the world's foremost medical hypnotist. Erickson was able to deal effectively with even highly resistant clients whom other therapists had been unsuccessful with. The technique Erickson used is often referred to as *pacing*.

In this context, pacing means *meeting the other person where he or she is, reflecting what he or she knows or assumes to be true, or matching some part of his or her ongoing experience.* In other words, you are pacing another person to the extent that you are in agreement or alignment with him or her, or bear some likeness to him or her. You'll recall that this is similar to the definition for rapport. Pacing, therefore, is a specific technique for establishing rapport with virtually anyone. It is being or becoming like that other person so that you can get that person's attention and friendship and help.

There are many ways you can pace another person. You can pace a person's mood, body language, and speech patterns (including rate of speech, tonality and volume, and the words, phrases, and images a person uses). You can pace another person's beliefs and opinions. You can even pace another person's breathing patterns. Remember the law of requisite variety: the wider your own range of behavior, the more easily you can pace a wide variety of behavior in someone else, or a wide variety of personality types. This part of the book will show you how to pace people to establish rapport with them.

I Like You Because You're Like Me

It may not be fair, but it is nonetheless true that people like people who are like themselves. We want to commune with people who are like us, who see the world in the same way we do, who have similar likes and dislikes. We choose our friends from among those acquaintances who make us feel comfortable with ourselves. And who could possibly make us feel more comfortable than someone very much like ourselves? Studies reveal that people also tend to hire people who are like themselves. Many years ago, psychologist William Sheldon at Columbia University postulated that people are attracted to and even choose to marry people with similar body types.[3]

Another phenomenon, which is linked to persuasion, is that when a person likes you, he or she tends to want to agree with you. Pacing is a way of being like another person, the probable outcome of which is that the other person will like you and will feel psychologically impelled to agree with you. The formula (admittedly oversimplified, but nonetheless useful) is this: If I am like you, you will like me; and if you like me, you will want to agree with me.

Matching the Other Person's Mood

Every mood seeks companionship. Just as misery loves company, so also do cheerful, enthusiastic people want to associate with similar people. When some people wake up in the morning, they're fairly subdued. Other people, in contrast, have their eyes pop open and their bodies pop up—they're wide awake and alert before their feet hit the floor.

The world is not necessarily split evenly between these two sorts, but if one day you come to work wide awake, bright-eyed, and find yourself face-to-face with your still sleepy, still puffy-eyed associate—whose consent you just happen to need quite badly—it might be an especially good idea to tone down your excessive vigor, initially at least.

In the same way, if you're the phlegmatic one, find some way of pepping yourself up. Your sluggishness probably will not endear itself—or you—to a person who enjoys seeing the same kind of spark in someone else that he or she personally possesses. William James explained how this can be accomplished through the cyclical interplay of feelings and actions: "Action seems to follow feeling, but really action and feeling go together; and by regulating the action, which is under the more direct control of the will, we can indirectly regulate the feeling, which is not."[4]

He continued, "Thus, the sovereign voluntary path to cheerfulness, if our spontaneous cheerfulness be lost, is to sit up cheerfully, to look round cheerfully, and to act and speak as if cheerfulness were already there. If such conduct does not make you soon feel cheerful, nothing else on that occasion can."[5] In other words, act as if you're cheerful and you'll bring about the real thing. Or, as some people are fond of saying, "Fake it 'til you make it."

Are you really happy this morning, or are you just dealing with your anger in a positive way?
Drawing by Stevenson © 1980 The New Yorker Magazine

When you change your behavior you change your experience. The actor, Dustin Hoffman, often goes out into the world in the role of the character he is playing to better understand the part. Thus, for the title role of *Tootsie* he dressed up as a woman and went out onto the streets of New York City. When he was preparing for the role of Ratzo, the down and outer in *Midnight Cowboy*, he went down into the bowery of New York's lower east side to participate in that experience. Charleton Heston, an actor of a very different sort, put it this way: "If I can find the outside of the character, the inside will come."

It may be easier to lower your energy level than to increase it, but the critical factor remains the same: People like people who are like themselves.

If you're the chipper one and endeavor to influence a far less enthusiastic individual, add common sense to the techniques of pacing. Eight o'clock in the morning may not be the time to approach a haggard family member, co-worker, boss, or subordinate. Wait for a more appropriate moment—after lunch, perhaps—when he or she is more responsive. But if it's eight o'clock and there is no time to waste, understand the risk if you present yourself in a way that does not consider how the other person feels. Your idea might face stiff resistance—not because your proposal is weak, but because your mood is out of sync with that of the other person. For example, say you slap your sluggard colleague on the back so his or her coffee spills, and remark that you've already jogged eight miles. Then you suggest that your respective departments collaborate on the new sales program. You may get a look of pure hatred—and you probably won't get any cooperation.

The importance of pacing is this: When you pace another person, you are in effect saying, "I'm like you. You're safe with me. You can trust me." Pacing is a way to establish trust and credibility. There are, of course, other ways of establishing credibility, such as presenting one's status (as boss or expert, for example) or using appropriate language (speaking with authority). But pacing is an exceptionally reliable method that is applicable to nearly all encounters.

Pacing—whether pacing of mood or some other behavior—is not always easy to do. But you can at least approximate the other person's behavior, if it is within a normal range of behavior. Patricia Fripp, a nationally known speaker, shares this anecdote:

I am very, very impatient, and I walk quite fast. One day, I met one of my elderly customers walking down the hill outside my office.

I was as usual in a great rush, in a hurry to get to work or go to the bank or get somewhere else. But he wanted to walk—stroll, really—with me. He was over seventy years old and couldn't possibly have kept up with my pace.

I thought for a moment, and decided to actively calm myself down. I suddenly refused to be my normal impatient, frenetic self. And I ended up enjoying the more leisurely pace, the walk, him, and myself.

I've learned that we are much more in control of our feelings than we think. I hear people say, "Oh, I can't help it; that's just the way I am." Now that's silly. That's the way they have programmed themselves to be. Well, they can unprogram themselves. And they ought to do it.

Frederick Perls, the founder of Gestalt therapy, expressed similar sentiments: "Once you have a character, you have developed a rigid system. Your behavior becomes petrified, predictable, and you lose your ability to cope freely with the world with all your resources."[6] Perls vigorously urged people to get rid of their characters, the inflexible, programmed part of the way people see themselves and present themselves.

This statement of Perls was quoted to an executive who once complained about having to get a subordinate's cooperation by dropping a level or two below his own rather frenetic level of activity. However, he was subsequently convinced that this doesn't pose an insoluble conflict. Someone who drops, or even rises, a beat or two to accommodate someone else's rhythm need not become glued there. In fact, after initially pacing another person you may even end up raising or lowering that person's level until it matches your own.

The phenomenon here is simple: When you're in step with another person, the next step you take the other person is apt to follow. It seems paradoxical at first, but one of the best ways to change another person's behavior is to first synchronize yourself with some aspect of his or her behavior (pace it) and then change yourself. In hypnosis, this is called *leading*, a concept that will be developed later.

As you can see, matching moods is another example of the law of requisite variety. If you are programmed into a rigid "character," you don't have enough flexibility to meet people at their own level. But if your range of moods is broader and more adaptable than the other person's, you can not only meet the other person on his or her level and establish rapport—you can also then move off in a new direction. If you first match them, people will follow your lead.

Body Language

As psychology professor Albert Mehrabian points out, "Our silent messages may contradict or reinforce what we say in words. In either event, they are more potent in communication than the words we speak."[7] "Indeed," says Mehrabian, "in the realm of feelings, our facial expressions, postures, when our words contradict the silent messages contained within them, others mistrust what we say—they rely almost completely on what we do."[8]

Social psychologist Clara Mayo and Rosalyn Lindner, of the National Jury Project, which helps attorneys in the intricate art of picking juries free of sexual and racial biases, echo Mehrabian's findings. In response to challenge questions, say Mayo and Lindner, attorneys should be looking not for what prospective jurors say but what they do. For example, in the courtroom, where it seems socially unacceptable, people will deny harboring racial prejudice. Even specific questions—"Have you ever worked with members of the particular minority group in question? Or known them as neighbors? Or served with them in the military?"—might elicit less than honest answers. "The manner of answering," Mayo and Lindner warn, "may reveal more than the words."[9] When a prospective juror begins to pause or fidget (clear indications of tensions), lawyers should probe more deeply.

Mehrabian arrived at the reasonably safe generalization that nonverbal behavior far outweighs the impact of words when the two seem contradictory. "In other words, touching positions (distance, forward leaning, or eye contact), postures, gestures, as well as facial and vocal expressions, can all outweigh words and determine the feelings conveyed by a message."[10]

Facial expressions carry the greatest weight (55 percent); vocal expression (tone of voice) is next (38 percent); and words, third (7 percent). To elaborate, "If the facial expression is inconsistent with the words, the degree of liking conveyed by the facial expression will dominate and determine the impact of the total message."[11]

So when you pace mood in another person, be aware that words and body language can give different messages and that the body language you use is the most important factor in establishing rapport.

How to Speak Body Language

In recent years, many books and articles have been written about the importance of body language. Much of this literature, especially in popularized versions, has focused on the meanings of various postures, gestures, and so on. It's easy to become lost in the maze of conflicting theories and observations. Here it is important only that you be aware of another person's nonverbal behavior and respond to it appropriately. In general, pacing—aligning your own nonverbal behavior with that of the other person—is an appropriate response and is an effective strategy for establishing rapport at the body level. Pacing body language, in fact, is something that we all do unconsciously much of the time. It occurs naturally when people are in rapport. Consider, for example, this quote from the *Harvard Business Review*:

> In moments of great rapport, a remarkable pattern of nonverbal communication can develop. Two people will mirror each other's movements—dropping a hand, shifting their body at exactly the same time. This happens so quickly that without videotape or film replay one is unlikely to notice the mirroring. But managers can learn to watch for disruptions in this mirroring because they are dramatically obvious when they occur. Instead of smooth mirroring, there will be a burst of movement, almost as if both are losing balance. Arms and legs may be thrust out and the whole body posture changed in order to regain balance.[12]

Sometimes, in moments of deep rapport, you will observe a scene like the one between Adrienne and Conrad (they're in love, as you can tell from the hearts surrounding them):

Studies by psychologists Condon and Sander support this view of rapport. Condon writes:

> The sharing (sustaining together) of movement and/or posture between (people) . . . provides constant ongoing information about the nature and degree of that relationship, an ongoing waxing and waning across the dimension of love and hate, of closeness and distance. Many of the nuances in a relationship are conveyed by the subtle rhythms in movement and posture sharing. . . . The more two (individuals) share movement or posture together, the greater the rapport between them. Such rapport contributes to a sense of acceptance, belonging, and well-being.[13]

Spontaneous and unconscious pacing is, in fact, a characteristic of all human interaction. Some researchers refer to this phenomenon as "interactional synchrony." The process, it seems, starts at birth. In the early 1960s Condon and Sander studied films made at the Child Development Unit of the Boston University Medical Center, films that showed the "correspondence between analysis of the soundtrack of (an) adult's speech and body movements of (an) infant."[14] In some cases, the infant was barely twelve hours old. Other researchers have found that newborn babies orient themselves to sound, preferring the sound of the human voice, especially a woman's voice. They prefer to gaze at faces rather than other objects; their eyes follow a turning human face, and they may imitate certain facial gestures.

In *Beyond Culture*, Edward T. Hall cites studies on the innate nature of the "synchrony" phenomenon, studies in which movies "taken in a variety of settings and circumstances, reveal that when two people talk to each other their movements are synchronized.[15] This synchronization, Hall points out, occurs in barely discernible ways: an eyelid blinks or a finger curls in synchrony with a particular word sound or voice stress. In other circumstances, two bodies may move entirely in synchrony with one another, "as though the two were under the control of a master choreographer."[16] Furthermore, observes Hall, "Viewing movies in very slow motion, looking for synchrony, one realizes that what we know as dance is really a slowed-down, stylized version of what human beings do whenever they interact."[17]

Communication is Like a Dance

So pacing may be a survival mechanism, one that we learn in our first interactions with other human beings. As Hall puts it, "Being in sync is itself a form of communication."[18] Perhaps it is the most important form of communication there is.

Spontaneous pacing of body language occurs when you are in rapport with other people. This interactional synchrony occurs, for the most part, below the level of conscious awareness. But what happens when it doesn't occur spontaneously? The non-verbal message you are communicating to the other person is, "Right now, at this moment, I'm different from you." Sometimes this difference does not affect the outcome of the interaction. But at other times it could mean the difference between getting cooperation and getting resistance. Consider the following example in which Adrienne, Conrad, Atherton, and Mr. Griggs are having a meeting. Mr. Griggs is the boss, and the others are trying to convince him that their respective ideas are ones he should accept.

Look for a moment at the nonverbal messages each participant is sending to Mr. Griggs. Whether you attach any intrinsic meaning to Atherton's crossed arms or to Conrad's casual resting of his hand on his chin, you can see that the message that both men are giving Mr. Griggs is, "Right now, at the body level, I am different from you." Adrienne, however, is saying, "Mr. Griggs, I am like you." All other things being equal, Adrienne probably has the best chance of getting Mr. Griggs to go along with her idea. The message she is sending him is being received at the unconscious level. The message is "I'm like you. You can trust me." Mr. Griggs probably wouldn't be able to say what he likes about Adrienne, but that in no way lessens the impact of her actions.

Sometimes communication at the nonverbal level is the only way to make contact with other people. In 1970, dance therapist Janet Adler successfully broke through the barriers surrounding the tightly sealed world of two autistic children. Two-year-old Debra and five-year-old Amy had no verbal language, nor had either ever experienced a relationship with another human being.

On the recommendation of a therapist, each child began seeing Adler two or three times a week. After first repeatedly rejecting her, the children began to allow Adler to move into their world. Eventually the distance between her and them lessened. Filmed sessions show Adler at work. She explains what quickly became obvious: Communication was possible in only one way—through the body. "I tried to enter their world," she explains, "and speak their language by reflecting their movements."[19]

The children ultimately chose "mutuality over isolation" until mutual trust existed at the body level. "There were sometimes magnificent moments when our bodies were in a heightened synchrony; in these moments, we were saying something very important to each other. For both Debra and Amy, this was just the beginning, but for the first time, they had each experienced a relationship with another human being."[20]

The film begins with Adler's imitation of the children's uncoordinated and seemingly purposeless movements. It ends with their following her, alternately prancing, romping, and virtually floating around a dance studio with intention and direction. The film serves as the best possible testimony to the positive effects of pacing and the affirmative results it can produce.

How to Speak the Other Person's Verbal Language

Pacing verbal communication strongly influences the depth of rapport you establish with another person. By changing this one aspect of his behavior, the owner of an answering service dramatically increased the subscription rate. After becoming familiar with pacing, he began to match the rate of speech of the people who called in for information. Because his only contact with prospective clients amounted to one or two phone calls, he had to make each conversation count. If the potential customer spoke rather quickly, he spoke rather quickly; if slowly, then slowly. This one simple change, he reported, resulted in a 30 percent increase in his subscription rate.

Serious problems can occur if you fail to take into consideration the rate of speech of the person you want to influence. Have you ever seen someone from New York City try to do business with someone, for example, from Mobile, Alabama? If the consequences weren't frequently so unfortunate, the process itself would be humorous. The New Yorker, vibrating with frenetic intensity and talking rapidly, is trying to close the deal so he or she can catch the 1:25 flight back home. The Southerner, relaxed and speaking slowly, is wondering what's wrong with this strange creature. The New Yorker is frustrated by the other's unhurried languor, while the Southerner is put off by the frenzied pace of the New Yorker. The one wishes the other would speed up and get on with it, while the other would like to slow down and take it easy. Each may have good ideas from which the other could benefit, but the process of communication lacks harmony. It might well interfere with their trusting each other enough to complete the transaction. If either had the perceptiveness to understand what was going on and the flexibility to meet the other at his or her own level, the transaction could proceed much more smoothly. Whether one speeds up or the other slows down is really not important. What is important is they meet on common ground long enough to complete the transaction.

David Woodward, formerly the Western Regional Sales Manager for Raychem Corporation, tells this story about a sales call he once made on a corporate vice president. Dave walked into the prospect's office expecting to make a dynamic presentation that he hoped would lead to a nice piece of business. The man behind the desk, however, gave him a start. Dressed in tight jeans, pointy cowboy boots and a string tie, he looked more like an actor in a grade-B western than a corporate executive. He stared at his boots propped up on the desk and drew out his words in a halting monotone.

Taking his cue, Woodward slumped down in his own chair just like the "cowboy" and forced himself to match the other's torpid speech. "It damned near killed me," says the robust Woodward, "but after 20 minutes, I got him to sit up in his chair, establish semi-eye contact, and talk a little faster." By the end of the meeting, the vice president had become so enthralled with Woodward that he introduced him to the entire company. Woodward left with the business.

Pacing volume is also a useful tactic. Someone who speaks softly will appreciate someone else who speaks softly. Likewise, someone who speaks loudly will often have more respect for you—will recognize a kindred spirit—if you match the volume. As a matter of fact, on occasion you might even want to exceed the other's volume in order to get him or her to speak more softly. A friend shared this rather bizarre experience:

> I once had a client who I suspect must have been certifiably insane. He was a screamer. He'd pound tables and jump around and scream and holler. Everybody who worked for him walked on eggshells in order not to disturb him and set him off on a rampage.
>
> I was at his house one night and we were talking business, still sitting after dinner at opposite ends of a long dinner table. As usual, he soon began to yell and pound the table, screaming about how worthless and stupid his employees were. I tried to calm him down but nothing I said seemed to have any effect. It was embarrassing.

> So I decided that since I'd tried everything else I might as well try pacing his hostility. I began screaming, too, but I was careful to scream with him, not at him.
>
> "You're absolutely right, Charlie!" I screamed. "We ought to fire everybody and start all over again. We should even burn down the office and build another one! As a matter of fact, we shouldn't just burn it down—we should blow it up!"
>
> I was really getting into the role now, hollering at the top of my lungs while beating on the table with both fists.
>
> At the other end of the table, Charlie had fallen completely silent and his face was pale. He looked at me and put his hands out, "Calm down, Burt. Just calm down and let's talk this over."

Paradoxically, by giving other people a reflection of themselves—and even exaggerating that reflection somewhat—you can often cause them to modify their behavior. This is a higher risk tactic, however, especially with people who behave at the extremes, and should therefore be used judiciously.

What Burt did here was risky, but he minimized the risk by making sure he got into alignment with Charlie's hostility. Had he yelled at Charlie rather than with him, the level of discussion probably would have raised the ceiling.

Some people, such as Charlie, find that they can control people by going out of control (which is mostly an act—they are usually in complete control of themselves and the situation). What they depend on is the predictable behavior of those around them. As long as other people react to them according to their plan—in Charlie's case, the plan is to go out of control in such a way that other people will acquiesce and placate him—that, in effect keeps the "out of control" person in control. And in fact most people do react to Charlie's blustery behavior by treading softly around him and pleading with him to calm down, usually to little or no avail. In pretending to lose control, Burt interfered with Charlie's game plan. He disturbed Charlie's system, so to bring it back into balance Charlie was forced to play the role of placater.

You may have seen the same pattern of behavior in children. A child may learn to scream and throw temper tantrums in order to control other people. But if you or another adult pace that behavior by also throwing a tantrum (with the child, not at the child), a miraculous and amusing calm can set in. The child's astonishment can then give way to humor—and the pattern is broken.

The message here is this: If you want to change someone else's behavior, the best approach is to change your own. The resulting change in the system will then often prompt the other person to change him or herself in order to re-establish the balance, and with it the illusion of control.

The words, phrases, and images other people use give you important information about the inner worlds they inhabit. By pacing this aspect of their speech, you are telling them that you understand them and that they can trust you. "I like that guy—he speaks my language," is an idiomatic expression that means, "Hey, I like him. He's OK. He's like me, I can trust him." So when you're talking with other people, it's a good idea to incorporate as many of their words, phrases, and images into your conversation as you comfortably can. Don't mimic another person's accent or speak a jargon you don't have mastery of—such an attempt would probably backfire. But you should be sensitive to his or her level of vocabulary and imagery and try to reflect it as closely as you comfortable can. This also means avoiding in your own speech any jargon that the other person doesn't understand.

Putting someone in the position of either appearing stupid or feeling stupid will only cause resentment. Thus confronted, an individual may reject your idea not because it is weak but because he or she may not understand it in the way it has been presented. Pedantry blocks rapport, so unless the other person shares your expertise and the corresponding jargon, avoid it.

Having requisite variety means having more options with which to encounter other people, especially other people whose behavioral styles are quite different from your own. Having requisite variety means being able to avoid those styles that inadvertently turn other people off.

Having the flexibility to use words, phrases, and images familiar to other people is important. If you listen carefully to the language other people use, you will know what words, phrases, and images they feel at home with. In the cartoon, for example, the catcher is talking but the important message is the bewildered look on the pitcher's face.

© 1980 Sidney Harris — Discover

Incidentally, as the world gets smaller, more and more contacts arise among businesspeople who really do speak different languages. Most will speak some English, so you can usually be sure of being able to communicate the technical side of your business.

But it will help the interpersonal side of the transaction if you try to learn even a few words of the foreigner's language. It is a gesture of goodwill that is appreciated. Also, body language can be very useful in bridging the gap. However, gestures are not international. Shaking your head can mean either Yes or No, in different cultures. Stay alert to the context of gestures, and ask for clarification if you need it.

Before my partner made her first business trip to Japan two years ago, she did some homework. She learned a few key words and phrases, the proper way to bow and when to do it, the etiquette of presenting and receiving business cards, and the names of the most popular Japanese baseball players. Since she already liked sushi, she didn't have to worry about that. When she returned, I asked what made the trip successful. Here's what she said, "My Japanese hosts were very surprised and also very pleased that I knew a few words and that I'd taken the time to actually learn something about their culture and ways of doing business. And when they invited me to lunch and I chose sushi from their list of options, they were delighted."

Speak other people's language, and you'll find that they respond to you much more positively. They'll appreciate your effort, and you'll dramatically increase your effectiveness in getting their cooperation and support.

Pacing Beliefs and Opinions

Milton Erickson tells of an incident involving his small son. As you read this story, keep in mind that one goal of pacing is to be able to lead the other person in the direction you want him or her to go. Observe how skillfully Erickson accomplishes this:

Three-year-old Robert fell down the back stairs, split his lip, and knocked an upper tooth back into the maxilla. He was bleeding profusely and screaming loudly with pain and fright. His mother and I went to his aid. A single glance at him lying on the ground screaming, his mouth bleeding profusely and blood spattered on the pavement, revealed that this was an emergency requiring prompt and adequate measures.

No effort was made to pick him up. Instead, as he paused for breath for fresh screaming, I told him quickly, simply, sympathetically, and emphatically, "That hurts awful, Robert. That hurts terrible."

Right then, without any doubt, my son knew that I knew what I was talking about. He could agree with me and he knew that I was agreeing completely with him. Therefore he could listen respectfully to me, because I had demonstrated that I understood the situation fully.

Then I told Robert, "And it will keep right on hurting." In this simple statement, I named his own fear, confirmed his own judgment of the situation, I demonstrated my good, intelligent grasp of the entire matter and my entire agreement with him, since right then he could foresee only a lifetime of anguish and pain for himself.

Erickson here truly operates in unison with his son, establishing a strong sense of credibility in his son's eyes by reflecting what Robert already knows to be true, namely that his mouth hurts awfully and will probably go on hurting forever.

Next Erickson leads Robert to a different and more productive awareness of his predicament. He does this by focusing Robert's attention on the amount and the quality of the blood on the pavement, while at the same time linking the blood to something Robert considers important, namely the quality of the blood: "That's an awful lot of blood on the pavement. Is it good, red, strong blood? Look carefully, Mother, and see. I think it is, but I want you to be sure."

Here Erickson is leading Robert, the objective being to place his attention on something other than the pain. Erickson continues:

However, we qualified that favorable opinion (of the quality of the blood) by stating that it would be better if we were to examine the blood by looking at it against the white background of the bathroom sink. By this time Robert had ceased crying, and his pain and fright were no longer dominant factors. Instead, he was interested and absorbed in the important problem of the quality of his blood.

Erickson then proceeds to lead Robert farther away from the trauma and the pain by wondering if Robert will be fortunate enough to require as many stitches as he could count:

In fact, it looked as if he could not even have ten stitches, and he could count to twenty. Regret was expressed that he could not have seventeen stitches, like his sister Betty Alice; or twelve, like his brother Allen; but comfort was offered in the statement that he would have more stitches than his siblings Bert, Lance, or Carol. Thus, the entire situation became transformed into one in which he could share with his older siblings a common experience with a comforting sense of equality and even superiority.[21]

By skillfully pacing Robert's belief that it hurts and will go right on hurting, Erickson has first paced his son's pain and then led the boy's mind away from the pain to the quality of his own blood and the prospect of having more stitches than he can count, or at least more stitches than his siblings. This is the art of Erickson's style. It is also the art of persuasion: validating something other people already know to be true, and then leading them to consider and finally to accept other possibilities.

The misconception many people have about persuasion is that it is possible to convince people of something they do not at some level already believe or have some need to believe. In his *Techniques of Persuasion*, J. A. C. Brown puts it this way: "It would appear that the main lesson to be drawn from our present study . . . is how very resistant people are to messages that fail to fit into their own picture of the world and their own objective circumstances, how they deliberately (if unconsciously) seek out only those views which agree with their own.[22]

Thus our attempts, however well-intentioned and correct, to enlighten others are jeopardized from the start if we begin by informing the misguided that they are in error. The most likely result of such a course is defensiveness. It's useful at times to keep in mind that when you are dealing with another human being you are dealing with perhaps the most dangerous creature on the earth—one who will die (or kill) to defend his or her beliefs. To a great extent (some would say completely), our reality is made up of our beliefs; therefore, to tamper with people's beliefs is to tamper with their reality. Tread lightly. Or better, pace the belief. Then lead with your own suggestion.

Of course, you should not pretend something that you don't believe, or compromise your integrity. But you can usually find some way of validating another person's beliefs or experience of him- or herself. As Thomas Jefferson once said, "In matters of principle, stand firm like a rock; in matters of opinion, flow like a river." Find a point of agreement on which to build your case, then if necessary move into areas of disagreement or misunderstanding. It is much easier, and much more effective, to move from agreement to agreement than from disagreement to agreement. If there's nothing in the other person's point of view you can legitimately pace, then pace the feeling. The statement "If I were in your place I'm sure I'd feel the same way you do," is always going to be true. If you had the other person's genetic and personal history you would certainly feel exactly the way he or she does, because you would be that person. I'll address this subject in greater depth in Part Four, "Dealing with Resistance."

Pacing Breathing

Another subtle but potent way of being "in sync" involves breathing. Nothing is more vital to all humans than the voluntary and involuntary inhaling and exhaling of air. But we seldom think about it. In *Frogs Into Princes* Richard Bandler and John Grinder present an example of pacing breathing. Bandler recalls:

> Once I was in a Napa State Mental Hospital in California, and a guy had been sitting there for several years on the couch in the dayroom. The only communication he was offering me were his body position and his breathing rate. His eyes were open, pupils dilated. So I sat facing away from him at about a forty-five degree angle in a chair nearby, and I put myself in exactly the same body position. I didn't even bother to be smooth. I put myself in the same body position, and I sat there breathing with him. At the end of forty minutes, I had tried little variations in my breathing, and he would follow, so I know I had rapport at that point. I could have changed my breathing slowly over a period of time and brought him out that way. Instead I interrupted it and shocked him. I shouted "Hey! Do you have a cigarette?" He jumped up off the couch and said, "God! Don't do that!"[23]

This incident offers an excellent, if somewhat unusual, example of pacing and then leading a person to a different level.

The synchronization of breathing is also one of the oldest rapport-building techniques on record. In some variations of Tantra Yoga, where the objective is to achieve a spiritual merging, two individuals hold each other gently and breathe together until the apparent barriers separating them drop away and the experience is one of unity, the inspiration and expiration of a single organism, not two separate entities.

Although not often used in a business context, this particular form of pacing, used skillfully, can be a powerful way to gain an intuitive understanding of another person. Melinda Henning, a sales training consultant from the San Francisco Bay Area, tells this story:

> A few years ago I was doing some telephone sales training for a client. Our original agreement was that I would consult on a combination of set fee plus a performance bonus for increases in sales. After an initial three month feasibility study it became apparent to me that the results we would be able to get would substantially increase the production of his salespeople. So I decided to schedule a meeting with him to suggest a different compensation plan—one that would pay out less in fees but more for increased performance.
>
> When we sat down I started the meeting by reviewing our performance to date, which indicated a promising future. The discussion was genial but there was something not quite right that I couldn't quite put my finger on. We reviewed the numbers and he praised my performance but I felt that there was something bothering him. The discussion just kind of stalled and I couldn't figure out what was wrong. Then I decided to start breathing in unison with him, and as I did so I noticed that my breathing, like his, was high in the chest and quite rapid. I began to feel very uncomfortable. Then suddenly, it dawned on me why our discussion had stalled. "Are you afraid of something?" I asked him. "Yes!" he said. "I'm afraid I won't have the cash flow to meet your expenses."

After finding out what the problem was, Melinda was able to reassure him that he had very little to worry about and that, far from creating a negative cash flow, her efforts would very likely result in a positive cash flow. It was her sensitivity to his feelings, augmented by her being able to empathize with him through pacing his breathing that enabled her to perceive the nature of the problem and address it appropriately.

The Next Step: Leading

When you've achieved rapport with another person, the other person is apt to follow your lead—i.e., when you're in step with another person, the next step you take the other person is apt to follow. You can think of the general pattern in this way: Pacing is doing something similar to what the other person is doing; leading is doing something different from what the other person is doing. When you're with another person, you're either pacing (doing something similar) or leading (doing something different) with respect to whatever behavioral dimension you're considering. There are no other possibilities.

If your primary objective is simply to get along with the other person, then pacing some aspect(s) of his or her behavior is sufficient. But if your objective is to persuade, to bring the other person to a new awareness, then you must lead. In general, the best strategy is to pace first, then lead. Meet the other person where he or she already is, and then suggest some new options. This approach works more frequently and more effectively than any other. Sometimes it is not appropriate to lead quickly, and sometimes it may be wiser to back off and not try to lead at all. Different situations will dictate different approaches. But as a rule, the pace/lead strategy is an effective way to persuade.

How to Test for Rapport

Before you attempt to lead the other person, it is a good idea to find out if you have effectively established rapport. This can be done unobtrusively at the nonverbal level by first synchronizing with some aspect of the other person's body language, such as posture. Mirror the other person for a short time (a couple of minutes should be sufficient, initially). Then change your posture and wait to see if the other person responds. The response could be a move to a mirror position of your new posture, or it might simply be a shifting, a "settling in" on the part of the other person to restore balance to the system. What you are looking for here is a congruent, or complementary, response by the other person. If this occurs, it will tell you that you have rapport at the nonverbal level and that this might be a good time to lead verbally, to suggest the idea you want the other person to consider.

You might also test your lead at the verbal level. In sales jargon, this is sometimes referred to as a trial close—the asking of a leading question to find out if the prospect is receptive. Such an interaction might go as follows:

You :   (Shifting your body) John, we've agreed that the problem here is that absenteeism and tardiness are costing us a lot of money, both directly and indirectly.

John: (Shifting slightly in your direction, partially mirroring your posture) Yes, it's become a serious issue. We've got to do something.

You: (Sensing that you now have rapport and are in agreement and alignment at both the verbal and nonverbal levels) What I'd like to suggest is that we consider going on flex time to decrease the problem. What do you think about the idea?

If John continues to agree with you, then keep leading. Keep elaborating on your idea, asking for confirmation from John at each crucial step.

However, if when you test for rapport the other person does not respond as you'd like, either verbally or nonverbally or both, then resume pacing. For example:

You:	(Shifting you posture) Are we in agreement that the problem is really one of time and not money?
John:	(Remaining in the same posture) I'm not so sure. The time schedule is a problem, of course but I'm not sure we could fit the cost into this year's budget.
You:	(Resuming your former posture, partially mirroring John) So, we agree that the time schedule is a problem that needs to be addressed, but you're not sure we can afford to do it right now. Well, maybe we need to think this through a little more deeply. What do you suggest?

The general rule here is that if the other person resists your lead, go back to pacing and look for new opportunities to lead, after agreement and/or alignment has been reestablished. The pace/lead model might look like the following diagram:

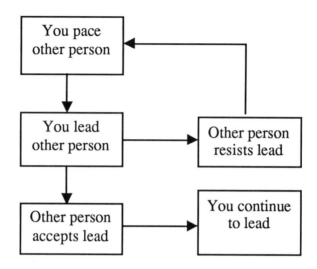

Most interactions involve a continual process of pacing and leading, back and forth, until a satisfactory outcome is achieved (or the discussion is ended).

When Not to Pace

Whenever you're doing something that isn't working stop what you're doing and do something else.

I learned this the hard way when I was just learning about pacing and was trying out my new "skill" on just about everyone I encountered. One evening a friend and I were walking down Geary Street in the San Francisco theater district when a man stumbled out of an alley and started babbling incoherently at us. I figured this would be a good time to try my new pacing "skill." So I turned to him and started babbling back. He looked at me strangely, took a step back, put his hand in his pocket and brought it out with a knife in it. He opened the knife and came toward us threateningly. At this point I realized that pacing wasn't working and I'd better do something else fast. So I threw open my arms and said to him, "You're absolutely right! And besides, there are three of us." He stopped in his tracks and seemed to be pondering what I'd just said. My friend and I decided to leave, which we did quickly.

The moral of this story: Don't pace aberrant behavior unless you really know what you're doing. Also, when you're doing something that isn't working, stop and do something else. This is why it's useful to have enough variety in your responses for your purposes. In general, it's a good idea not to pace something that you assume the other person is not comfortable with, or accepting of, in himself or herself. Don't pace an accent, or stuttering, or limping, or asthmatic breathing. Avoid tics and other nervous mannerisms that might call attention to what you're doing. In the matter of beliefs and opinions, don't agree with anything that violates your cherished principles. It's not necessary; there is usually enough in another person's belief system to align yourself with for the purpose of establishing common ground.

You may also want to avoid pacing behavior that could be construed as resistant or non-accepting. For example, should you pace another person when she or he is sitting rigidly with crossed arms, apparently resistant to your idea? Opinion is divided on this question. Some experts believe you should always avoid pacing resistant behavior. Others think that by pacing resistant behavior and then leading to more open behavior, you can model what you want the other person to do. It's likely that the most prudent tactic would be to do whatever is consistent with the situation. If there's tension in the air, it might be wiser to pace something other than closed body language. If, on the other hand, there are no indications that the other person is resisting, then pacing closed body language could be appropriate. Sometimes you may think a person is resisting if his or her arms are crossed, for example, when it's just that there are no arms on the chair, or it's cold in the room. Gestures or postures do not have universal meaning; behavior is highly idiosyncratic (although at the same time being highly patterned within the individual). The general rule, in any event, holds: If what you're doing isn't working, change your behavior and do something else.

Pacing Written Communication

Up to this point we've talked about pacing people either in person or on the phone. The same principles apply to written communication, whether it be letters, memos, formal presentations or electronic mail (email). The idea is to identify where the other person is coming from and get in sync with him or her. You can't pace body language or rate of speech but you can pace the other person's beliefs, opinions, or expectations. You can also pace the other person's tone, or mood—formal or informal, light-hearted or serious, etc.

This is especially important in email exchanges, where the only thing the other person has to respond to are the words on the screen. Here, using the words, phrases, and images of the other person can be critical in establishing rapport. It's easy to misunderstand another's intentions when you don't have nonverbal and para-linguistic behaviors (such as volume, pitch, tonality, rhythm, etc.) to guide you in interpreting the other's emotions. (Although one of the conventions that has developed in electronic communication is the use of symbols to represent emotions. These emotional icons, or "emoticons," as they're sometimes called, are intended to reflect your emotions/intentions when the words alone might be misunderstood. For example, "Just kidding" might be something like :>} . . . "I'm so sad" could be :>{ . . . and so on). This can get out of hand, though, and become an excuse for careless writing. Keeping in mind the general guideline for rapport—getting in sync with the other person—you'll probably have more success with emoticons and other such devices with people who use them with you first.

Another of the problems I've observed, especially in electronic communication, is that we sometimes feel that it is safer to express our darker side in writing, since we don't have to deal with the immediate reaction and physical presence of the other person. This is especially true when the other person may be someone we've never even met in person, but have just encountered in a chat room or a newsgroup or mailing list.

Again, the best advice is to follow the general rule of pacing—looking for areas of agreement in what the other person is saying; reflecting in a positive way what the other person has written to you; and aligning with what the other person is expecting from you. In written communication it is critically important to give the other person the benefit of any doubtful intention and to look for and find ways to be supportive. Keep in mind that what you put out over the Internet can be replicated and distributed to millions of people in a matter of hours, and your darker moments can come back to haunt you. As motivational speaker Jim Rohn likes to say, "Be real nice to people." With respect to rapport—especially e-rapport—that's real sage advice.

Outcomes of Pacing

When you pace another person, you are communicating that you are sharing a common experience. You're saying—whether literally or figuratively—that you speak the same language, you're on the same wavelength. Pacing also creates a harmonious climate for your ideas and suggestions because what you're doing is accepting the other person. And your acceptance will most likely lead to his or her acceptance of you. Pacing reduces resistance, because no matter what the other person does, you can synchronize with it. You can "go with the flow" and then redirect it. Most importantly, when you pace another person you're communicating the very important message that you're alike. And people tend to like people like themselves and feel a need to agree with people they like. In other words, when you pace another person you are creating rapport, and with it an atmosphere of trust and credibility.

When you pace another person, you are also doing some significant things to and for yourself. Pacing, done effectively, will take your attention off yourself. One of the greatest benefits of pacing is that you don't have to worry about what to do with your hands or feet, how to sit, how fast to move, at what rate to speak, or what level of vocabulary to use, and so on. You simply take your initial cues from the other person and get "in sync" with him or her.

Pacing also enables you to share the other person's experience, which is what empathy is all about. When you act like another person, you begin to feel many of that person's feelings. You begin to know intuitively what to suggest and when to make the suggestion.

Pacing also prepares the way for leading. When you're in step with another person, the next step you take he or she is apt to follow.

That is why pacing is one of the most powerful secrets of the power of suggestion.

Another View of Pacing

One of the most frequent concerns people have about pacing is that it's manipulative, that it's mechanical, that surely the other person will know what you're up to and will become offended. The answer to this is "Yes, maybe, probably not." It's certainly the case that anything done unskillfully or for nefarious purposes is likely to cause unwanted repercussions. The idea behind pacing is not to take advantage of someone but rather to get in alignment with him or her for the purpose of producing a more effective outcome, whether the context is sales, teamwork at work or at home, or simply getting along with another person because that's what feels best.

For most people this explanation suffices to ease their concerns about the ethics of pacing. However, there is another concern about pacing that is not usually voiced, but is nevertheless an issue that should be addressed. Namely, does pacing produce a genuinely closer relationship between two people or does it somehow remain a "technique" that one person is "using on" another? The answer, again, is Yes and No. It depends on how you use it and it depends on how deeply embedded the skill of pacing is. If it's something you do consciously, there will no doubt be an aspect of mechanicalness about it—until you learn how to make it part of who you are and what you do with other people as a matter of course. Until it becomes a habit. How long does that take? I've heard it said that if you practice something for 21 days in a row you will probably have it—whatever it is—ingrained. Perhaps. It might take longer, it might not take that long. The important thing is that you practice it regularly. Look for ways to get in alignment with what other people are saying or doing. Look for ways to synchronize with others.

A Variation on the Theme

One of the most profound ways to establish a deep bond of rapport with another person was developed by Dr. Jesse Tuffman, a clinical psychologist whose work with couples includes this exercise:

He suggests that one of the individuals imagine that he or she has no way of receiving information from either the external or internal worlds except through the other person; that the only connection with any kind of experience is being channeled through the other person; that he or she suspend for the purpose of the exercise all attempts to evaluate, react, or in any way experience any thoughts or sensations that do not emanate from the other; that all experience is coming through from the other person. The desired effect is to produce a profound empathy.[24]

It's a form of pacing, to be sure, but it's pacing that eliminates any barriers between yourself and the other person. It's not manipulative in that there is no attempt to "do" anything to or with the other person. The only objective is to become the other person, to give up the separate identity. It's more than attempting to see things *from* the other person's perspective. It's actually seeing/hearing/feeling *with* the other person's perspective.

Prior to his working with couples in a therapeutic or personal growth setting, Jesse taught this approach to salespeople in many different fields and with results that he says multiplied their previous production by as much as seven or eight times.[25]

Rapport with Yourself

So far you've learned about interacting and gaining personal power with other people. A major theme has been that when people like you and feel comfortable with you they are more likely to respond positively to your influence.

Sometimes you need to influence—convince—yourself before you can effectively influence others. In order to be maximally effective with other people, it's important to have a good relationship with yourself. In other words, you need to have rapport with yourself.

It could be argued—as poets often do—that our natural state is to be in rapport with ourselves and that as we grow older we lose this connection We become more self-conscious and self-consciousness brings with it self-assessment. And negative self-assessment, whether it's self-talk, self-imaging or self-feeling—whether it's visual, auditory or kinesthetic—is detrimental to experiencing and exercising personal power. Perhaps this is another example of innocence—and paradise—lost. In any event we learn to interrupt this natural state and in doing so, block rapport with ourselves. Usually this is done in one (or more) of three primary ways, corresponding to the three primary ways we make sense of things:[26]

> Negative self-talk (auditory)
> Negative self-imaging (visual)
> Negative feelings about self (kinesthetic)

Let's look at each of these and discuss how to re-establish rapport with ourselves at each of these levels.

Negative Self-Talk: Stop It and Reframe It

Negative self-talk is one of the most insidious ways we block rapport and sabotage ourselves. It's a source of much misery in our lives and it's unfortunate that there is nothing, to my knowledge, present in our educational system to address this issue. When we hear our own negative self-talk, we need to stop it and pull ourselves out of its negative spiral. One simple strategy for doing this, and a favorite of cognitive psychologists, is to say STOP! as soon as we hear it. This will interrupt the negative self-talk and give us an opportunity to deal with it.

A simple yet effective way to deal with negative self-talk is to challenge it directly with positive self-talk. Art Rutzen, CEO of SDR Capital Management in San Francisco, is a former world class college wrestler and uses positive self talk to combat a tendency to get down on himself when playing tennis. If things are going badly for him, Art often motivates himself with a pep talk by saying things like, "You're better than this, Art. You can do this. You can beat this guy." He also encourages his tennis doubles partners and in much the same way. Not surprisingly, he also uses this same style with his business associates.

It's a simple strategy, but it's a time-tested and effective one. It simply requires that you be aware of your own internal dialogue, or monologue, and intervene when the messages are counter-motivational or counter-productive.

A more complex process is to reframe the negative self-talk. In *Learned Optimism*, his excellent manual for combating this problem and the tragic consequences of it, Martin Seligman outlines a strategy that can be used for reframing a negative outlook and the resultant pessimism that comes from such a view.[27]

The first step is awareness. When we are confronted with some kind of adverse situation we need to be aware of how we talk to ourselves. Some of us, when confronted by adversity, respond with pessimistic self-talk. We say things like, "It's hopeless. I'm no good at this—or anything else for that matter. Never have been. Never will be." This is the ultimate state of pessimistic belief and can lead only to despair and further ineffectualness.

According to Seligman the way out of this pessimistic trap is through appropriate attribution. In the example above, I'm attributing the cause of my condition to some deficiency in myself ("I'm no good at this") and then compounding that by telling myself that it applies to everything I attempt ("or anything else for that matter"), and that it will last forever ("Never have been. Never will be.") The foundation for a pessimistic world view is thus firmly established: the attribution is personal, it's permanent, and it's pervasive. One of the outcomes of this kind of pessimistic view is chronic depression.

To combat this pessimistic pattern Seligman recommends a frame that he calls the ABC model. It's a continuation of the initial awareness. Here's how it works:

> A stands for Adversity. This is the event that triggers the pessimistic response.

B is the Belief that is reflected in the negative self-talk (e.g., "I'm unlucky about this and everything else in life. I'm powerless to do anything about it. It'll always be like this.")

C is the Consequence of this belief. Invariably beliefs reflecting ill-fortune and powerlessness pervading one's life have an enervating effect and cause a further erosion of one's self-esteem and effectiveness.

Becoming aware of our individual manifestation of this ABC pattern is the first step to dealing with it.

The next step in dealing with this ABC trap is to add steps D and E to the process.

D stands for Disputation. When we notice ourselves engaging in negative self-talk we need to dispute the underlying belief.

Seligman identities four ways of disputing a debilitating belief:

1. *Marshalling evidence to the contrary.* For example, the belief that "I'm unlucky" can be disputed by bringing into awareness aspects of one's life that are positive: "I have a good job. My wife/husband loves me. I've been fortunate in that my health has always been good," etc. Also, "I know I've felt this way in the past and things haven't always turned out poorly. Sometimes things have even turned out for the best."

2. *Creating alternatives to the belief.* Maybe what happened had nothing to do with my being unlucky but rather has a different explanation.

3. *Examining the implications of the belief.* So what if it's true? What's the worst thing that could happen as a result? (In this case being congenitally unlucky is probably not a good

frame, since the worst thing that could happen probably always will. Therefore this is not a good option.)

4. *Determining the usefulness of the belief.* How useful is this belief? Does it serve me? When does it serve me? (Perhaps it serves to keep me out of poker games in which I have a tendency to lose a lot of money, in which case this belief is situationally useful.)

Seligman thinks that the first tactic—marshalling evidence to the contrary—is generally the best choice. It's easy and it's quick and doesn't require a lot of analysis.

Finally, the last step in the process is E.

> E stands for Energizing. When we're successful in disputing our negative beliefs, we feel energized and optimistic.

A step I would add to Seligman's process is pacing, to ensure that we have rapport with ourselves before engaging in the disputation. The reason for pacing oneself is the same as for pacing another: it smoothes the way for leading. Making myself wrong for my thinking is a potential mind trap that can be easily avoided by the simple addition of a pacing step. It helps "set" the frame. Here's how it works:

> *The negative belief*: I'm unlucky about this and everything else in life. I'm powerless to do anything about it. It'll always be like this.

> *The pace*: It's true that sometimes I'm unlucky.

> *And then the lead*: But this is true of everyone. It's part of life. And the good news is that it's also only temporary. Things always turn around.

> *The negative belief*: It affects every aspect of my life.

The pace: It certainly seems that way at
times—especially when I wake up at 4 o'clock in the
morning and start obsessing about it.

The lead: But in fact in many ways I'm very fortunate.
I've been blessed with good health. I'm an
intelligent person and I have an understanding wife
who loves me and whom I love deeply.

This approach used consistently should help you reframe
negative and pessimistic self-statements and lead to a more
positive and optimistic outlook. An optimistic outlook will in
turn energize you so that you will produce more positive and
powerful results—with yourself and with others.[28]

Seligman cites a study he did with life insurance agents at
the Metropolitan Life Insurance Company that concluded that
the more optimistic agents outperformed the less optimistic ones
by a substantial margin. The agents in the top half of the study
sold 56 percent more insurance than those in the bottom half.

Reframing Negative Self-Imaging:
The Swish Pattern

There are times when we deplete our personal power not by
our negative self-talk but by our negative self-imaging. We see,
in our mind's eye, previews of coming attractions and the
movies are not pleasant ones. In our external lives we have the
choice not to go to those kinds of movies, but in our internal
lives it's not so easy. How do we turn off these previews and
turn on movies that portend more pleasant realities?

In NLP there is a powerful technique for reclaiming the
screening room in your mind. It's a way of replacing the
negative image or picture with a positive one. It's called the
swish pattern.

The swish pattern can be likened to the Picture in Picture
(PIP) feature that many televisions have. This enables you to

have two channels on the screen at the same time—a large, full-screen picture and a smaller picture in one of the corners of the bigger picture. If something of greater interest comes on in the small picture (PIP) you can switch the image to the larger screen, causing what was on the larger screen to appear in the smaller window. The swish pattern works in much the same way.

When you want to rid yourself of a negative image, or images, in your mind, first create a picture of a desired state and then insert that desired state in the smaller window of your mental screen. This can be either a still image or a series of moving pictures. Then switch—or "swish"—the images so that the larger, undesired state, becomes small and the small, desired state, becomes large. Repeat this until you can make the interchange effortlessly. You can enhance the swish technique by adjusting the fine tuning on the picture. Make the positive image sharper, more vivid and more colorful, while making the negative image drab, washed out and less distinct.

Your ultimate objective is to have the positive image "take over" in your mind. When this happens you will carry around within you your own power-generating station. You'll choose which channel you want to watch rather than having unwanted channels beamed in by some insidious internal and debilitating process. This exercise dramatizes the fact that you are in control of the pictures in your mind, and it is therefore your choice which ones predominate.

Transforming Negative Feelings about Yourself: Form Counter-anchors and Then Collapse Them

Much of our personal power is dependent on our feelings about ourselves and our congruence with the messages we are conveying. Consequently, it's critically important that we pay attention to the messages we're communicating to ourselves so that we can project a strong sense of self to the person(s) we want to influence. Here's an easy way to test the thesis that positive thoughts strengthen and negative thoughts weaken.

Stand up and hold one arm out straight to the side. Think of something that's very negative to you and have someone try to push your arm down. Notice the result. Hold your arm out again and think of something that's very positive to you. This time when the other person tries to push your arm down, it's likely that he or she won't be able to do it, or at least not as easily as when you were thinking the negative thought.

One of the implications of this experiment is that the things we say to ourselves and the thoughts we have about ourselves have a powerful impact on the vehicle in which we travel, our body. Negative thoughts and feelings diminish both our physical strength and our personal power.

One of the most powerful techniques for dealing with a negative feeling is to exchange the negative feeling for positive feelings using anchors and counter-anchors. What you're doing is overwhelming the conditioned negative feelings with conditioned positive feelings.

Here's an example of how this might work.

> *Identify the negative feeling.* Let's say your negative
> feeling is fear. You're a salesperson and you dread
> making cold telephone calls.

> *Recreate the negative feeling and anchor it.* While
> you're experiencing that fear anchor it by touching
> your right ear with your left hand (best to pick
> something that you wouldn't do unconsciously to
> avoid triggering the anchor inadvertently). By
> touching your right ear you're creating an
> association in your mind so that when you touch
> your ear, you're creating a stimulus that produces a
> conditioned negative response. Test the anchor by
> firing or triggering it (in this case, touching your
> right ear with your left hand). You want to be sure
> that the anchor is producing the negative response
> that you want to overwhelm. If you test it out and

have a negative response, then the anchor is working. If you test it and you don't have a negative response, you haven't set the anchor properly. Go back to the beginning, recreate the negative feeling and set the anchor again for that feeling. The test for the anchor is getting the negative feeling.

Recreate and anchor a sequence of positive feelings. Now think of something that always causes you to have a positive feeling. Anchor that feeling by touching your right hand to your right knee. Think of another positive feeling and again anchor it with your right hand to your right knee. Do it again with another positive feeling. Repeat this process, stacking up four or five positive feelings until you reach the point at which when you touch your right knee with your right hand you experience a flood of positive feelings.

Collapse the anchors and overwhelm the negative feeling. The next step is to rid yourself of the negative feeling by overwhelming it with positive feelings. You do this by triggering both the positive and negative anchors simultaneously. The effect is to create such a surge of positive energy that it overwhelms and neutralizes the negative energy.

Summary

R apport is "a relation marked by harmony, conformity, accord, or affinity." In persuasion, it is important that you be able to establish a strong bond of rapport with the person you want to influence.

Pacing may be thought of as holding a mirror up to people so that what they see, hear, or feel is consistent with their experience of themselves and their reality. Pacing involves getting into agreement or alignment with, or bearing a likeness to other people in a way that communicates, "You can trust me. I'm on your side. I'm like you." People tend to like people like themselves, and will want to agree with people they like.

Pacing not only has a powerful impact on other people, it also has a dramatic effect on you. By pacing others you are in a sense getting inside their bodies and minds, so that you come to have an experience similar to theirs. Effective pacing enables you to achieve a profound level of empathy with other human beings.

A major objective of pacing is to so closely match another person's ongoing experience that the distinction between what that person is doing and what you are doing becomes blurred (at the unconscious level). This enables you to successfully lead him or her into new areas of experience. When you're in step with another person, the next step you take he or she is likely to follow.

Suggestions for Practice

1. Many people find that rate of speech is the easiest thing to pace initially. If you find it more comfortable, start with

people you know fairly well. Or pace strangers who call you on the telephone. Listen to the rate of their speech, and reproduce it in your conversations with them. Then, when you feel comfortable pacing their rate, pace the volume, then the tonality, etc. After a short while, you'll find that you can do this without even thinking about it. As a matter of fact, you'll probably find that, to a certain extent, you're already doing it with people. The goal is to be able to do it without conscious effort, so that it becomes an automatic part of your behavior, like driving a car or riding a bicycle.

2. People's speaking rates vary considerably. Some people speak slowly, pausing frequently to find the right words and phrases. Others speak rapidly and seem to have no trouble at all finding the words—the only difficulty they seem to have is in getting the words out quickly enough. If your style is to speak more slowly, you might have more difficulty pacing a rapid speaker, but with practice it can be done. You'll find that your thought processes alter as you change the rate of your speech. This is one of the most effective ways you'll ever find to get inside another person's mind. After you've become adept at pacing, you'll begin to notice that you've become much more adept at anticipating what the other person is about to say. What happens when this occurs is that you have so attuned yourself to the other person's way of speaking, thinking, and behaving that you are able to engage in a form of mind-reading. The two of you will have become one, so to speak.

3. As with any new skill, pacing is something that comes easily after you practice it systematically. It's a good idea to practice one thing at a time—mood, body language, rate of speech, and so on. After you become proficient at pacing, you will be able to do it without thinking about it. It will come naturally and easily. Every day, practice pacing some aspect of another person's ongoing experience. Take one thing at a time until it becomes natural and comfortable for you.

4. As you watch television, practice sitting in the same position as someone you're watching. Notice how your feelings and experience of yourself change as you assume different postures. Talk shows are good for this exercise, because you often have an opportunity to pace several different individuals.

Part One
Notes

[1] See W. Ross Ashby, *An Introduction to Cybernetics*, (New York: Methuen, 1956).

[2] The caveat here is that requisite variety obtains when all things are equal: If you have requisite variety with respect to your boss, for example, you may not always be able to control the outcome of the situation, given that she has positional power in the organization. However, behavioral variety is a wondrous thing and will often trump even positional power.

[3] William H. Sheldon, with the collaboration of C. Wesley Dupertuis and Eugene McDermott. *Atlas of Men: A Guide for Somatotyping the Adult Male at All Ages* (New York: Gramercy, 1954).

[4] William James, *The Moral Equivalent of War and Other Essays*, ed. John K. Roth (New York: Harper and Row), p. 51.

[5] James, p. 51.

[6] Frederick S. Perls, *Gestalt Therapy Verbatim* (Moab, UT: Real People Press, 1969), p. 7.

[7] Albert Mehrabian, *Silent Messages* (Belmont, CA: Wadsworth, 1971), p.56.

[8] Mehrabian, p. 40.

[9] Denise Grady, "Picking a Jury," *Discover*, January 1981, p. 39.

[10] Mehrabian, p. 45.

[11] Mehrabian, p. 43.

[12] Michael B. McCaskey, "The Hidden Messages Managers

Send," *Harvard Business Review*, November-December 1979, p. 147.

[13] William S. Condon, "An Analysis of Behavioral Organizations," *Sign Language Studies*, Winter 1976.

[14] William S. Condon and L.W. Sander, "Neonate Movement Is Synchronized with Adult Speech: International Participation and Language Acquisition," *Science*, January 11, 1977, p. 99.

[15] Edward T. Hall, *Beyond Culture* (New York: Doubleday, 1976), p. 72.

[16] Hall, p. 72.

[17] Hall, p. 72.

[18] Hall, p. 71.

[19] "Looking for Me." 1969. A film documenting Adler's work with autistic children. Center for Media and Independent Learning, 2000 Center Street, Berkeley, CA 94704..

[20] Ibid.

[21] Jay Haley, *Uncommon Therapy: The Psychiatric Techniques of Milton H. Erickson, M.D.* (New York: Norton, 1973), pp. 189-190.

[22] J.A.C. Brown, *Techniques of Persuasion: From Propaganda to Brainwashing* (New York: Penguin Books, 1963), p. 309.

[23] Richard Bandler and John Grinder, *Frogs Into Princes* (Moab, Utah: Real People Press, 1969), p. 80.

[24] Personal communication.

[25] Of course in a sales context there's more involved than simply achieving profound levels of empathy. In a classic study, "What Makes a Good Salesman," published in the *Harvard Business Review*, Herbert M. Greenberg identifies two key success factors, empathy and ego drive. Ego drive in this context means simply getting gratification from selling, from the process of persuading someone else to do something.

[26] In NLP these three ways or modes of perception are often referred to as "representational systems." This concept is explored more fully in Part Two.

[27] Martin E.P. Seligman, Ph.D., *Learned Optimism*, (New York: Knopf, 1991), pp. 213-228.

[28] For some interesting variations on the concept of reframing negative self-talk, I highly recommend Robert Dilts' *Sleight of*

Mouth. Dilts is one of the most prolific and most profound of writers on NLP and is always stimulating. In *Sleight of Mouth*, Dilts offers some 14 ways of reframing, some of which are variations on themes we've already discussed and some expand the technique to new areas of exploration.

PART TWO

The Art of Clear Communication

Misunderstanding can result when people automatically assume that others think as they do.
—Robert Sommer, *The Mind's Eye*

This part of the book deals with an often-neglected aspect of communication: how people process information and attempt to make sense of things. In order to get other people to understand what you mean, you first need to understand *how* they understand, or at least how they try to understand. When you understand how other people process information, you can organize your communication in a way that "fits" their modes of perception. We're still going to be talking about pacing (and leading), but we'll be dealing mainly with less visible behavior, that which goes on inside other people.

In the second section of Part Two, we'll relate the information about how people understand to one of the most powerful techniques ever devised for ensuring mutual understanding and clear communication. This is the technique of active listening, pioneered in the early 1950s by Carl Rogers. We'll then take a step beyond active listening to probing for hidden meanings.

Understanding How
Other People Understand

S cience writer Gordon Rattray Taylor recalls his earlier
years:

When I was in school, I vividly remember, I had no
difficulty with geometry, because I could recall the
figure and derive the proof of the theorem from it. The
fact that the square on the hypotenuse of a triangle
equals the sum of the squares on the other two sides
has remained with me because I recall the diagram. On
the other hand, algebra and calculus I found extremely
difficult, and only those parts which could be
graphically represented could I retain. I distinctly
remember the flash of illumination which struck me
when, after an incomprehensible discussion of
algebraic formulas for a parabola, the teacher drew a
diagram on the blackboard, and showed how it came
about.[1]

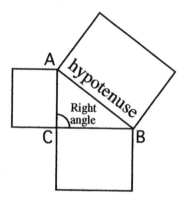

The square of the hypoteneuse equals the sum
of the squares of the other two sides.
Or, $AB^2 = AC^2 + CB^2$

"I myself am strongly visual," confesses Taylor, "and I certainly find it hard to follow the writings of philosophers, which are highly conceptual."[2] Visualizers, he explains, have difficulty forming abstract concepts and communicating with people who do.

In *The Mind's Eye*, psychology professor Robert Sommer concludes that visualizers inhabit a sensory world that differs from the world of other people. Sommer explains the difficulty he faces in dictating letters or notes when his secretary is on vacation.

> Although I know the work will be done as soon as she returns, the picture of her empty desk and lonely typewriter discourages me. I have never felt comfortable having my work typed by an anonymous steno pool. Nor do I like giving instructions about car maintenance to a service manager in a sparkling white smock when the work is to be done by someone else. I feel better if I can see the mechanic who will be doing the job so I can picture the person making the needed repairs. There are also large printed signs on the wall prohibiting customers from entering the service area. Not only am I unable to picture the mechanic doing the work, I also have no visual picture of the repair area or the tools used. So much of our alienation from the world of machines and technical processes results from an inability to picture what happens.[3]

In contrast to the visual, a self-described "primarily auditory person," writer Howard Gardner, argues that dictation rather than typing or writing by hand improves a writer's output: "When I speak (into the machine), I appear to be following the dictates of an inner voice—that is, I don't see any words in front of me, but I hear what I am about to say and find myself virtually transcribing the sounds of the words with my tongue."[4] In his conversations with others, Gardner has learned that there may be different cognitive styles involved in dictation. For example, "Those who are more visually oriented appear to see a sentence in their minds—sometimes visualizing a whole paragraph as they construct it."[5] Gardner said, "In my own auditory imagination, I can hear some of what came before and some of what is to come, but little more."[6]

In contrast to visual and auditory people, is the kinesthetic individual, a person with not only a heightened sense of touch but heightened sense of emotion, of intuition, of "felt" inferences and reactions that seem to transcend the normal cognitive process. The sculptor Rodin was such a person. As art critic and historian Kenneth Clark notes, Rodin's primary process was physical; his "instruments of power and communication were his fingers."[7]

Once, when asked to explain what jazz is, Louis Armstrong is said to have replied, "If you can't feel it, you can't understand it." And tennis star Andre Agassi, asked by interviewer Roy Firestone what it's like to be on center court at match point, replied:

> The only sense you have is feel, and it's internal. It's not ears, it's not eyes, it's not taste, it's feel. It's like your body . . . when you're about to hit the shot to win the championship . . . if you blew out your shoulder as you're about to make contact you wouldn't even feel it.

Most people in our culture have difficulty understanding the kinesthetic mode. This, no doubt, is a major reason why body and emotive therapies have enjoyed such popularity. We want to get back in touch with our bodies and our feelings, and we seem to need the help of professionals to do so. Perhaps this is because as children we were often punished for expressing our feelings, especially when those feelings went counter to the desires of our parents and other adult authority figures. And for safety or housekeeping purposes, small children are often admonished to "look, but don't touch."

The fact that different people process information in different modes is, of course, critically important in communication. Communication means different things to different people. Couples often go into counseling because of "communication problems" arising from their different styles and different understandings of what communication means. In a typical first interview, the counselor might turn to the wife and ask her what the problem is. She might reply, "He just never *listens* to anything I say." The husband, on the other hand, might complain that "She doesn't *look* at me when I'm talking to her." Or either might think the other unfeeling and uncaring because he or she is "not very affectionate or emotionally responsive." When a mismatching of perceptual modes is involved in the problem, the counselor would first want to make the couple aware of what's going on, to point out to them that each is asking something alien of the other. The next step might be to get each person to learn to communicate in ways that are meaningful to the other. In the case just mentioned, for example, the counselor might encourage the husband to pay more attention to what the wife is saying. The wife might be advised to establish eye contact with her husband more frequently, to "show" him that she's paying attention to him.

I'm sorry, but I can't carry on an intelligent conversation. I'm visual.
Drawing by Weber ©1979, The New Yorker Magazine, Inc.

Seeing Is Believing; Hearing Is Believing; Feeling Is Believing

Each of us has, at any one time, a dominant or primary mode of perception. Richard Bandler and John Grinder, co-creators of Neuro-Linguistic Programming (NLP), refer to the perceptual modes by which we process information as *representational systems*. They describe the process this way:

> When you make initial contact with a person s/he will probably be thinking in one of three main representational systems. Internally s/he will be generating visual images, having feelings, or talking to themselves and hearing sounds.[8]

How to Identify Perceptual Modes

One of the simplest ways to identify another person's dominant, or primary, perceptual mode (or representational system) is to pay close attention to the words, phrases, and images he or she uses. A person in a predominantly *visual* mode will tend to select words that reflect a visual bias: "I *see* what you mean," "That idea *looks* good to me," "All I want now is the *big picture*. . . We'll *focus* on the details later," "My *point of view* is . . ." and so on.

In an *auditory* mode, a person is more likely to select these kinds of words: "*Tell* me again what you mean . . . I'm not sure I *heard* you right the first time," "That *sounds* like a pretty good idea to me," "Let me use you as a *sounding board* for an idea I have," "Yes, that's *clear as a bell*," or "Something just went *click* in my mind."

When a person is in a *kinesthetic* mode, you might hear: "I have a *feel* for what you mean," "That idea just *feels* right to me," or "I can't quite *get a handle* on this concept," or "He's the kind of guy who can just *take* an idea and *run* with it," or "This is a *solid* idea."

Semantically, "That idea *looks* good," "That idea *sounds* good," "That idea *feels* good," (or "That idea is *solid*") all mean the same thing. But psychologically they involve entirely different processes. Identifying which mode is dominant for other people at any given time is an important element—both in understanding them and getting them to understand you.

Another way to find out which perceptual mode is preferred by another person is simply to ask, "How would you like this information presented to you?" People are usually aware enough of their own processes to give useful answers to this question. Some people, for example, will ask you just to tell them what you want. Others will ask you to write it down for them, perhaps including some charts and graphs or pictures they can look at. Still others might tell you that what they want to do is to get a good feel for the situation, that it's important for them to know they can trust you (such individuals may often say that they'd appreciate it if you "stay in touch" with them).

How to Get Others to Understand You

George, a management consultant, tells this story about one of his clients: It seems that a certain department in the organization was chronically late in meeting production deadlines.

George was called in to analyze the situation and recommend a solution. After talking with the department head and many of his key assistants, George discovered an interesting fact. The head of the department was devoted to written communications and was unwilling (or unable) to authorize anything without first having the request submitted in writing.

Some of his assistants had learned the secret of getting their projects approved, but many had not. The problem was further complicated by the fact that the department head was willing to have meetings with his staff and to give verbal agreements to ideas and suggestions during those meetings. But when it came time for him to act, nothing happened—unless the verbal agreement, together with a summary of the meeting, was given to him in writing.

When George discovered what was going on he had a meeting with the department head and his staff and informed them of his findings. He recommended that whenever anybody wanted the boss to do anything, that person put the request in writing.

The department head thought this was a fine idea, and although some of the staff grumbled about having to go to the bother of writing everything down, they nevertheless assented.

The department head was relieved, because his people were now committed to talking his language. (One of his assistants jokingly told him, "You even speak in memos.") And his assistants were relieved because now they had a workable strategy for getting projects underway more quickly.

In concluding his assignment, George wrote up his report for management, with a summary of his findings and recommended solution, had a copy of it framed, and sent it to the department head. At last report, the framed copy is hanging prominently on the wall in the department head's office.

In contrast, San Francisco consultant Lynn Lannon tells this client story:

> I was working with a Silicon Valley company with an office in Chicago. My client was concerned about problems in Chicago, which she described as decreased productivity and lack of teamwork. I went to Chicago to assess the situation and recommend an intervention. I did my usual round of interviews and data gathering and then pulled the team together to give them some feedback. I also thought, since I had them all together, that I'd do a bit of team-building.
>
> I talked about representational systems and described the three primary ways that we organize our perceptions and take in information—visual, auditory, and kinesthetic. I had them work in trios to help each other identify their primary, secondary, and tertiary ways of taking in information. Then I charted the results. Turns out that everyone's primary mode was either visual or kinesthetic except for one person—Joe, the manager. And he'd been making requests and giving information in *his* mode, which was auditory. This discovery was huge for this team.
>
> I talked with Joe about the value of using other people's perceptual modes and the impact a change in his behavior could have on the team. I suggested he do two simple things: (1) get a flipchart and keep it in his office so when agenda items came up he could write them on the chart and then use the chart in staff meetings [for the visual people] and, (2) make copies of those documents from which he normally read

information at staff meetings [so that the kinesthetic people would have something to hold]. I stayed in communication with him and he followed my suggestions (every consultant's dream!). The exciting thing was that there were immediate changes in the behavior and responsiveness of the team. And within one month the productivity problem had disappeared.

The message is clear: When you use the other person's perceptual mode, he or she will listen. You may need to expend a little more effort at the outset, but the extra effort probably will pay off and save you time in the long run. The other person will also appreciate the effort you've taken to find out how best to present your ideas to him or her. Taking the time to ask people how they would like information presented (whether formally or informally) is itself very persuasive and will help you get what you want more often.

Sometimes, however, it's not readily apparent which form of communication a person will respond most readily to. In such cases, you may need to use a trial and error approach. For example, if you're not sure whether another person is responding to you in a visual, auditory, or kinesthetic, mode, you might pause periodically to ask, "Does this idea *look* OK to you?" or "Can you *see* yourself using this system?" or "How does this *sound* to you?" or "Does it answer some of the *questions* you've been *asking* yourself?" or "I'd like to know how you *feel* about this program," or "Does this seem like something you can *run with*?"

If you don't get a meaningful response to the question presented in a visual mode, switch to the auditory. If that doesn't elicit much response, move to the kinesthetic level. One of the most frequent mistakes people make when they're presenting ideas to other people is to interpret a lack of a meaningful (to them) response as resistance, when in fact the other person's response may simply mean that you have failed to communicate in a way that he or she can make sense of. By having the flexibility (requisite variety) to switch from one perceptual mode to another, you will be able to reach more people more of the time, and they will more clearly understand what you want. This will enable you to get their cooperation and support more easily.

Consider another example, a hypothetical exchange between John and Sam. John is the buyer for an industrial firm, and Sam represents one of the firm's suppliers:

> John: Sam, I really don't see how this particular product can help our company. Can you show me why I should buy it?
>
> Sam: John, I don't know how I can say much more than I already have. It sounds to me like you just don't want to listen to a good idea.
>
> John: No, Sam, you're wrong. It's just that this idea doesn't appear feasible to me.
>
> Sam: John, I don't understand how you can help but hear the cash register ringing right now.
>
> John: Well, I guess I'll just have to pass on it for now. Maybe we'll take a look at it again the next time you're in.

Both John and Sam are revealing very important things about themselves to each other, but neither is aware of them. John is in a visual mode, while Sam is presenting information in an auditory mode. John wants to "see" how Sam's product can benefit him; Sam, however, is trying to make John "hear" the sound of the ringing cash register. John and Sam are failing to understand each other fully because they are organizing and communicating their perceptions in different systems. In effect, they're speaking different languages, even though neither is aware of it. The language of sight is quite different from the language of sound; and both are radically different from the language of feeling.

In the above example, Sam might have gotten his point across, and made the sale, had he detected that John's primary perception mode is visual. Sam's best strategy would have been to switch from an auditory to a visual presentation, at least initially. As it turned out, John was either unwilling or unable to make the necessary translation by himself. If Sam had been aware and flexible enough to alter his presentation from auditory to visual, he would have had a much better chance of effectively communicating his idea. For example, consider what Sam might have done:

John: Sam, I really don't see how this particular product can help our company. Can you show me why I should buy it?

Sam: Certainly, John. Look what happens when you combine it with Formula XL-38 here. Do you see the bubbling action now?

John: Yes, I do. The other stuff we've been using never did anything like that. That's pretty impressive. But will it do the job any better?

Sam: Well, let's find out. Watch what happens when we drop in a widget? (Drops in widget.) See how quickly it coats the widget?

John: Hey, that's really good!

Custom-Designing Word Pictures

Having correctly identified and made the necessary connection in John's visual mode, Sam might then proceed to a more sophisticated use of perceptual modes, that of perceptual overlap. This technique in sales is often referred to as "painting word pictures." The basic idea is to heighten other people's receptivity to an idea by presenting it so that they can see and hear and feel themselves experiencing the benefits of the idea. Perceptual overlapping allows you to "custom-design" the word picture to fit the primary and secondary perceptual modes of the person you are attempting to persuade.

For example if your boss Edgar is accustomed to processing information visually, and you can increase his awareness of the auditory and feeling dimensions, you are broadening the range of possible experiences for him, thereby heightening his receptivity to your idea. As J. A. Hadfield once observed, "Suggestion does not consist in making an individual believe what is not true; suggestion consists in making something come true by making him believe in its possibility."[9]

In the hypothetical example of John and Sam, for example, Sam might enrich John's experience by perceptual overlapping:

Sam: John, look at this process. See how quickly the coating goes on. And listen to the sound of the chemical reaction taking place. It's smooth and continuous, which tells you that the coating is going on evenly. You won't have to repeat the process later, as you've had to do so often in the past.

John: Wow! I would never have noticed that if you hadn't pointed it out. It does sound smooth. None of the herky-jerky gurgling that we get so often with Brand X.

Sam: That's right, John. And what's more, that sound you hear is also the ringing of your cash register, since you'll now be able to increase productivity. Which means that you'll be able to fill those back orders as well as take on new customers. How would you feel about that?

John: Sam, how soon can I get a shipment of this stuff?

This time Sam alertly switched his presentation to the visual mode, then overlapped the auditory, a system that is ordinarily secondary for John. What Sam accomplished by overlapping the visual with the auditory was to heighten John's receptivity by altering John's state of consciousness. Sam then completed the overlap in the feeling mode ("How would you feel about that?).

A hypnotist might say that Sam performed a mild trance induction with John. Sam's sales manager would probably say that Sam painted a word picture that caused John to want the product. Regardless of the terminology used, the outcome was mutually productive for both John and Sam. It was a successful communication. It was also a good use by Sam of pacing and leading. He alertly paced John's dominant visual mode and then led John by overlapping the auditory and feeling modes, thus ensuring that John would have a fuller experience of and appreciation for the benefits of product.

This approach is not only for persuasion. It's also an excellent way to expand another person's ability to experience an idea or situation.

For example, one day I was attempting to explain to a friend the concept of overlapping representational systems to enhance a person's ability to perceive and appreciate the richness of an idea. This particular friend happened to be in real estate sales at the time. She was, however, an extreme kinesthetic type and had difficulty relating to matters visual and auditory.

As we were discussing the concept of overlap, I asked her how she tries to communicate the attractiveness of a particular piece of property to a prospective buyer. "Don't you try to paint word pictures of some sort, so that the prospect can see, hear, and feel the benefits of this particular property?" "No," she replied. "I don't." "Well," I asked, "How do you try to get across the idea that he should buy this piece of property?" "I just have a feeling that it's the right thing for him and I tell him!"

This response prompted me to find out a bit more about her own preferences:

"Let me ask you this," I said, "Can you see yourself in your own living room right now?"

"No," she said, "I can't."

So I took a different approach. "Can you feel yourself sitting in your favorite chair in your living room?"

"Oh, yes," she said immediately.

"OK," I said, "As you're sitting there in your living room, enjoying the comfort of the chair, can you feel the warmth of the fire from the fireplace?"

"Certainly," she replied.

"As you're sitting there in your chair, enjoying the warmth of the fire, can you hear the sound of the logs crackling in the fire?" I asked.

"Yes," she said.

"OK, now that you're enjoying the chair and warm crackling of the fire, can you describe the room for me?"

At which point she described the couch, the pattern of the wallpaper, the pictures on the wall and bookcase full of books lining one of the walls. The point is, she had the ability to visualize but had to be led to it through her dominant kinesthetic mode.

Although she relied almost exclusively on the kinesthetic modality, my friend's experience is not really that unusual. Many communication failures occur because one individual relies heavily on receiving in one modality while the sender relies predominantly on delivering the communication in another. Perhaps you've witnessed two people unable to communicate with each other, when one finally throws up his hands in frustration and pleads, "I've tried every way I can to tell you what I mean without success. What do I have to do—draw you a picture?"

In fact, drawing a picture might be exactly what is needed. It could be a simple solution to what appears to be a hopeless problem. Pay attention to the way people make sense of the world and couch your communication in the same way. This is another example of pacing and is another important way to establish and maintain rapport with others.

Fortunately, my friend decided that real estate was not her true vocation and she subsequently got into counseling as a profession—a field where her feeling approach to matters was much better suited, because that's where her heart was.

Active Listening

I n the last section, we considered how different people organize their perceptions in the visual, auditory, and kinesthetic modes. We also explored how you can gain greater trust and understanding by being aware of these differences and then matching the other person's dominant perceptual mode. Now we're going to discuss a way you can combine this technique with another powerful method for promoting mutual understanding.

An important strategy for effectively communicating what you mean to another person and ensuring that you understand what the other person means is called *active listening*. The term grew out of psychological research and practice in the 1940s and 1950s. One of the earliest and best statements of the technique appeared in an article by Carl Rogers in the *Harvard Business Review* in 1952, entitled "Barriers and Gateways to Communication." In that article, Rogers identifies what he believes to be the major barrier to effective communication: our tendency to evaluate or judge the ideas of another person or group:

> Real communication occurs, and this evaluative tendency is avoided, when we listen with understanding. What does that mean? It means to see the expressed idea and attitude from the other person's point of view, to sense how it feels to him, to achieve his frame of reference in regard to the thing he is talking about. We know from our research that such empathic understanding—understanding with a person, not about him—is such an effective approach that it can bring about major changes in personality.[10]

The way to accomplish this empathic understanding, according to Rogers, is by following this rule: "Each person can speak up for himself only after he has first restated the ideas and feelings of the previous speaker accurately and to that speaker's satisfaction."[11]

To listen actively to another person means, then, that you learn to see, hear, and feel in the same way that he or she sees, hears, and feels. In effect, it is another form of pacing, of establishing and maintaining rapport. In his best-selling book, *Tuesdays with Morrie*, Mitch Albom relates how effectively his former teacher Morrie was in his ability to listen and to empathize with others, and how important this skill is in life:

> When Morrie was with you, he was really with you. He looked you straight in the eye, and he listened as if you were the only person in the world. . . . "I believe in being fully present," Morrie said. "That means you should be *with* the person you're with. When I'm talking to you now, Mitch, I try to keep focused only on what is going on between us. I am not thinking about something we said last week. I am not thinking of what's coming up this Friday. I am talking to you. I am thinking about you."
>
> I remembered how he used to teach this idea in the Group Process class back at Brandeis. I had scoffed back then, thinking this was hardly a lesson plan for a university course. Learning to pay attention? How important could that be? I now know it is more important than almost everything they taught us in college.[12]

Active listening, as described by Dr. Rogers, can be enhanced by pacing some of the other behaviors mentioned in Part One. By pacing, or synchronizing, your mood, body language, speech rate, and even breathing with the other person, you achieve strong rapport while maximizing mutual understanding. In addition, by matching perceptual modes you further ensure that you and the other person are communicating on the same level. Here's how you might practice active listening with a friend:

Friend: One of the things I'd like to do next summer is to learn how to SCUBA dive, because I think it would be interesting to float around underwater with those little critters. I've heard that it's like being on another planet down there, with lots of plants and things that you never see on land. The only problem is I can't swim, and I guess I'd have to learn how before they'd let me take lessons. I also wonder how much it's going to cost after getting certified. All that equipment looks real expensive to me. Also, I'd want to go diving with someone I know and trust in case I got into trouble down there. You know, sharks and things like that. What do you think? Would you like to learn how to SCUBA and go diving with me?

You: Well, friend, let me make sure I understand what you're saying here: You think you'd like to learn how to dive because you believe it would be interesting. But you'd have to learn how to swim first, which is a problem, and you also have some considerations about the cost of the sport. In any event, you'd like to dive with a buddy so you'd feel safer, and you want to know if I'd be interested, is that right?

Sometimes, when you paraphrase what you think the other person said, he or she will modify or clarify what was actually intended. In other words, you might not have misunderstood but, on hearing you restate it, the other person will realize that he or she has left something out. This often-quoted statement summarizes nicely the challenges of clear communication: "I know you think you understood what you think I said, but I wonder if you realize that what I said is not what I meant." Such is the challenge of clear communication.

Probing for Hidden Meanings

Active listening means listening empathetically so that you share, insofar as possible, the other person's experience, so that you receive his or her communication in precisely the way it is intended. This is an extremely useful practice. But there is a potential problem here, even if you do receive the speaker's intended meaning.

The problem is that people are not always completely aware of what they mean when they make statements. For example, in the statement, "I'm confused," the speaker is probably confused because he or she is not aware of something that he or she wants or needs to be conscious of. In this case, active listening is not likely to produce much more than an awareness of mutual confusion.

Most of us know (perhaps intuitively) that almost every sentence we utter omits something, either intentionally or unintentionally. And when someone speaks to us our choice is either to guess at what is missing or ask for clarification.

For example, in the utterance, "I'm confused," the omission, or deletion, involves what specifically the speaker is confused about, or in what way, specifically, the speaker is confused. The active listener will respond to and reflect the intended meaning, the speaker's state of confusion and will empathize with it.

But in such a situation even more is needed. Clarification of the specific nature of the confusion is needed, and this requires probing for hidden meanings.

A question often used to probe for hidden meanings is "Why?" This useful question often unearths a wealth of information about another person. But "Why?" can also be a potential barrier to effective probing. When someone is asked to justify a certain action or behavior, the form of the question is usually, "Why are you late?" or "Why didn't you get that report in on time?" or "Why did (or didn't) you do that?"

Such questions can be intimidating and may generate defensiveness. Coupled with an accusing tone, these questions strongly convey negative assessments.

"Why?" questions also have other potential limitations. One limitation involves the structure of the English language: A "Why?" question begs to be answered with a "Because" construction:

Q: Why are you confused?
A: Because I just don't understand.
Q: Why did you do that?
A: Because it seemed like the right thing to do.

Neither of these answers gives very much additional information.

A more effective approach to probing for unexpressed or hidden meanings is to ask "What?" questions: "What are you confused about?" or "In what way are you confused?" or "What, specifically, led you to do that?" or "What prevents you from doing this?" A "What?" question (and its variations, "Who?" "Which?" "When?" "Where?" and "How?") asked in a non-threatening tone will usually produce a specific response:

Q: What, specifically, are you confused about?
A: Well, I don't quite understand the exact relation here between A and B.
Q: What, specifically, led you to do that?
A: I thought that by doing it that way I could get the widget to fit better.

This is not to say that "Why?" is always an inappropriate question, nor that "What?" will always get you the specific information you want. But "Why?" will frequently result in generalizations, rationalizations, denials, or justifications. "What?" questions tend to produce specifics. For example, consider the following exchange:

Other Person: I've made my decision and it's final.
You: Why?
Other Person: Because I said so.

Then contrast it with this:

Other person: I've made my decision and it's final.
You: What could cause you to change your mind?

Or this:

You: Under what conditions might you change your mind?
Other Person: Well, I might change my mind if . . .

Here are some additional examples of how you might ask "What?" type questions:

Other Person: I'm not sure I need any right now.
You: What, specifically, aren't you sure about?

Other Person: I can't do it now.
You: What prevents you from doing it now? What's the worst thing that could happen if you did it now?

Other Person: Call me back in a month or so.
You: In what way will the situation be different in a month?

Other Person: I don't know. (expressing confusion or uncertainty)

You: If you did know, what do you think your
                answer would be?

Other Person: I can't afford it.
You: Under what circumstances do you think you
                could afford it?

Other Person: I don't believe in it.
You: What specifically don't you believe in? What
                could cause you to change your mind?

Other Person: I'm not interested now.
You: When do you think you might be interested?

Other Person: Maybe after the first of the year.
You: How will the situation be different then?

Summary

People organize their experience in three perceptual modes: the visual, the auditory, and the kinesthetic (odor and taste are used less frequently). Psychologists Richard Bandler and John Grinder have observed, in their work with Milton Erickson and others, that each of us has, at any time, a dominant perceptual mode, or representational system, to which the others are secondary.

In Western culture, for most people most of the time, the visual mode is primary. The expressions "Seeing is believing" and "I saw it with my own eyes" are indicative of the importance we attach to visually processed information.

The next most frequently used perceptual mode is the auditory. In an auditory mode, a person attends to the tonal qualities (sounds) of the information being processed, or constructs dialogues to organize his or her perceptions. These dialogues may be silent, internal ones, or they may be uttered aloud. Often, people having conversations with themselves are not consciously aware of what they're doing. In contrast to the visualizer, who is creating mental pictures, the person in an auditory mode is continually talking to himself or herself.

The least dominant (although certainly not the least important) perceptual mode, at least in the Western world, is the kinesthetic. People who are kinesthetically oriented tend to organize their perceptions primarily around their feelings. They have a "feeling" about things. When they reach out and touch someone it's a way for them to connect emotionally with others.

Of course, almost everyone has access to and uses all these perceptual modes some of the time, regardless of what his or her own particular bias is. What is important to note, however, is that this phenomenon of (unconscious) bias exists. As an effective communicator, you should recognize this process, understand it, and use it in your dealings with others. By so doing, you can dramatically increase the effectiveness of your communications.

By using active listening techniques, you can reach closer mutual understandings with others. Active listening involves a reflection back to other people of what you understand them to be saying. By combining active listening with an awareness of perceptual modes and other pacing techniques, you can help ensure that you see, hear, and feel what the other person is experiencing.

To move beyond active listening, to probe for hidden meanings, it is necessary to ask questions. "What?" questions produce more specific responses than "Why?" questions, which often result in defensiveness or generalizations.

Suggestions for Practice

1. In your conversations with clients, colleagues, and friends, and while listening to the radio or watching television, pay attention to the words and phrases people use to describe their experiences. Try to identify their dominant perceptual modes.

2. Keep a notebook to jot down words and phrases that indicate perceptual modes.

3. Practice using the same words and phrases as other people in your conversations with them. Vary this practice by choosing different words while remaining within the same perceptual mode. (E.g., if the other person uses the phrase, "I can't *see* the relevance of this," you might say, "So, this doesn't *look* right to you?")

have just said, or have intended. Remain in their dominant perceptual mode while doing this. You might also pace some of their behavior(s) to strengthen the bond of rapport you are creating.

5. Whenever someone says something important that you don't fully understand, probe for the hidden meaning by asking "What?" questions. Vary this by asking "Why?' questions to determine the difference in responses.

Part Two
Notes

[1] Gordon Rattray Taylor, *The Natural History of the Mind* (New York: Dutton, 1979), p. 215.

[2] Taylor, p. 215.

[3] Robert Sommer, *The Mind's Eye* (New York: Delacorte Press, 1978), p. 23.

[4] Howard Gardner, "On Becoming a Dictator," *Psychology Today*, December 1980, p. 14.

[5] Gardener, p. 14.

[6] Gardener, p. 14.

[7] Kenneth Clark, *The Romantic Rebellion* (New York: Harper & Row, 1973), p. 334.

[8] Richard Bandler and John Grinder, *Frogs Into Princes* (Moab, Utah: Real People Press), pp. 14-15.

[9] J. A. Hadfield, *Passages* (Winchester, MA: Allen & Unwin).

[10] Carl Rogers and Roethlisberger, F.J., "Barriers and Gateways to Communication," *Harvard Business Review,* July-August 1952, Reprint Review Series No. 21073, p. 25.

[11] Rogers and Roethlisberger, p. 26.

[12] Mitch Albom, *Tuesdays with Morrie: An Old Man, a Young Man and Life's Greatest Lesson*, (New York: Doubleday), pp. 135-136.

PART THREE

The Art of Persuasion

My most brilliant achievement was my ability to be able to
persuade my wife to marry me.
—Winston Churchill

In Part Two, we discussed perceptual modes and the importance of recognizing them in others. We also discussed using perceptual modes to make yourself more clearly understood and to heighten other people's receptivity to your ideas and suggestions.

In this section, we'll discuss decision strategies, so that you can identify them in others and use them to present your ideas in ways that are virtually irresistible.

We'll also explore one of the most fascinating and controversial techniques associated with the work of Bandler and Grinder—the use of anchoring to elicit the kinds of responses you want from other people.

The section on embedded suggestions shows you how the almost invisible presence of these language forms can make the difference between getting your ideas accepted or rejected. And it will also show you how to take control and remain in control of a conversation.

How to Get What You Want

"Ask and you shall receive." This advice is as good today as it was 2000 years ago. Why, then, does it sometimes seem so difficult to follow? Many explanations have been offered for our reluctance to ask for what we want. Sometimes we don't know what we want and don't want to appear foolish by making an incoherent request. And sometimes we know what we want but are afraid of the consequences of asking: we might be told that what we want is unrealistic, unacceptable, inappropriate, or unavailable. In short, we might be rejected.

The fear of rejection is not unrealistic. But effective communicators learn how to handle it. Noted sales trainer Art Mortel has observed, "You can be successful to the extent that you can tolerate failure." In other words, people need to re-evaluate failure, to see each No as just one more step toward an eventual, and inevitable, Yes.

The National Association of Manufacturers once did a study to find out how many times a salesperson was told No before the average sale was made. The study revealed that, on average, the prospect said No (or some variation such as "Call me back after I've had a chance to think about it") five times before he or she finally said Yes.

The life insurance industry has commissioned similar studies. Here the ratio is even higher: The average sale is made after the seventh rejection. No wonder only about one in ten life insurance salespeople makes a lifetime career of this arduous profession.

This doesn't mean that you should badger people until they give up—rather you should stay in communication, responding appropriately to each rejection. As sales trainers often emphasize, a rejection can be a disguised—or unconscious—request for more information. Combining respectful persistence with effective probing questions will often uncover the additional information that is required to dispel the resistance.

Persistence, then, is the key. Rejection is simply a necessary step to acceptance. Failure is a part of, not apart from, the path to success.

How to Come Up with a Good Idea

There are a couple of useful guidelines to keep in mind when you want to persuade someone of something. First, know exactly what you want, or at least what range of outcomes you'll be satisfied with. Second, people do things for their reasons, not for yours. So it is critically important that you find out enough about another person's reasons to be sure that you do in fact have a good idea to present to him or her.

A "good idea" is defined here as one in which the benefits to the other person outweigh the disadvantages. A useful way to determine whether you have a good idea or not is to do what Benjamin Franklin is reported to have done when confronted with a difficult decision. He would take a piece of paper and draw a line down the middle of it. At the top on one side of the line, he would write "Pro" and on the other side, "Con." Under "Pro," he would list all the reasons he could think of for going ahead with a particular course of action. Under the heading "Con," he would list all the reasons for not going ahead. In other words, he would list all the advantages (benefits) and all the disadvantages. If the advantages outweighed (subjectively, in his mind) the disadvantages, then he would go ahead with a good idea. But if the disadvantages outweighed the advantages, then he would consider the idea bad and would not act on it.

You can go through a similar procedure before presenting your idea to another person. Pretend you are the other person and, from his or her point of view, list all the pros and cons. If the pros outweigh the cons, then you have a good idea. If the cons outweigh the pros, however, you've got a problem: You need to either ask for less or offer more, so that the pros will come to outweigh the cons.

Let's assume that you've gone through this process, and you're convinced that, from the other person's point of view, you've got a good idea. The next step is to figure out the best way to present your idea so that the other person will accept it. If you can accurately identify and use the other person's decision strategy, you will be able to present your idea in a way that is almost irresistible.

Identifying Decision Strategies

Much has been written about the decision-making process. The classical model of how decisions should best be made goes something like this:

1. Analyze the problem or situation.
2. Generate some alternative solutions.
3. Pick one of the alternatives.
4. Implement the chosen alternative.
5. Monitor the results of that alternative.

In fact, however, the way people actually make decisions is highly individual. It is therefore important to understand how the person whose decision you want to influence makes this kind of decision. So, you'll want to know his or her decision strategy. A decision strategy, as it is defined here, is *the process (usually unconscious) a person typically goes through in making a certain kind of decision.* An individual may have several decision strategies for different kinds of decisions, but generally has only one strategy for each category of decision, such as buying cars, hiring employees, or approving budgets.

For purposes of simplicity and applicability, I'm dividing decision strategies into three phases (modified from the work of Bandler and Grinder):

1. *Motivation.* In this phase a person becomes interested in considering making a decision. The person is "deciding to decide."

2. *Decision.* Once motivated, the individual in this phase decides on a particular course of action (such as buying a particular car, hiring a particular employee, or approving or disapproving a budget). Note: The decision *not* to do something is also a decision and can give you just as much useful information as the decision to go ahead with a particular course of action.

3. *Verification.* Here the individual verifies that his or her decision was or was not a good one. When the individual regrets the decision, it's often referred to as "buyer's remorse."

To elaborate on this model, consider the first phase, motivation, with respect to a process with which you are probably familiar, buying a car. Some people are motivated to consider looking for another car only when prompted by urgent necessity; the old car is breaking down. Other people are motivated by long-range considerations and consistently plan ahead. In about a year, the car will begin to be a maintenance nuisance, so it's now time to start looking for a replacement, while the old one still has resale value. And a few people are impulse motivated; they see a shiny new red convertible, and they have to have it—now.

With respect to the decision phase, some people examine every conceivable alternative. Others need only two or three alternatives to choose from. Some people talk it over with others to get third-party opinions; others prefer to make the decision by themselves. Certain individuals need to get their hands on every piece of documentation and research they can find. Others are satisfied with simply finding a good, credible source that will recommend a particular course of action. And some people mull over the decision for weeks, months, or even years. Others will make the decision very quickly.

In terms of perceptual modes, some people are especially concerned with how a particular product or course of action "looks" to them, or how they will look in the eyes of others if they choose one alternative over another. Some people are more concerned with whether a particular choice will answer the questions they have been asking themselves, or what people will say about the decision. And still others are primarily concerned with how they or others affected by the decision will feel about it.

The verification phase is equally individual. Some individuals typically experience buyer's remorse, whereas others almost never do.

Clearly, the possibilities are limitless when you consider all the combinations and variations in decision strategies. Trying to decide how to approach a given individual might therefore seem almost hopelessly complex. And it would be, if it weren't for the fact that almost everyone is a creature of habit. Once a person develops a particular way of doing something, he or she tends to stay pretty much with that pattern. The person modifies the pattern only to accommodate changing circumstances or to stay interested in the process. The changes may involve either simplifying or complicating the process of decision making.

"No matter how obscured or distorted decision making may be in practice . . . there is a necessary underlying order to the procedure by which a decision is made."[1]

In order to identify another person's decision strategy for the kind of decision you want to influence, you need to develop as much information as you can about how that person has made similar decisions in the past.

You can get such information from a variety of sources. The person who will be making the decision is an obvious choice. But his or her associates are also extremely useful, and in some cases are even more reliable than the decision-maker.

Sometimes you may not even have direct access to the decision-maker, so you will have to get the information from other sources. For the moment, though, assume that you have an opportunity to talk with the decision-maker before making your presentation.

What you will want to do in this interview is to gather as much information as you can about what he or she wants, needs, fantasizes, hopes, dreams, likes, dislikes, fears, loves, hates—all this is useful information and will give you much valuable information that you will want to incorporate into your presentation. But most important of all, you will want to determine his or her decision strategy. This will tell you, more than anything else the person might say, what process he or she will probably use in considering your idea.

An analogous approach is the way in which human resource professionals are trained to evaluate a candidate for a job. The interviewer will ask the candidate why he or she wants the job, what he or she will do for the company, what his or her ambitions are, and so on. The candidate, of course, will tell the human resource person everything he or she thinks that person wants to hear.

The interviewer, however, will note the remarks of the candidate and will then proceed to gather as much information as possible about the candidate's job history—who he or she worked for, when, and for how long; how the person got along with others, whether he or she was punctual, energetic, creative, enthusiastic, diligent; and whatever else might be important for the job under current consideration.

The interviewer knows that patterns tend to repeat. If the candidate was a good employee during the last few jobs, then the chances are that he or she will do a good job the next time. If the candidate had problems in the past, then those problems (if part of a pattern) will probably replay themselves on the next job.

In other words, the interviewer will look for employment patterns and will make the valid assumption that the patterns will persist. You can do the same thing in identifying decision strategies. Look for the patterns in past decisions of the kind you want to influence and use those patterns in designing your presentation.

To identify the various phases of a person's decision strategy, you might ask the following questions:

1. *Motivation*

    What prompted you to consider buying your last _____?
    How did you decide you wanted or needed _____?

2. *Decision*

    What factors went into your decision to _____?
    When you made your last purchase of _____, what
        were the deciding factors in your mind?
    How did you reach the decision to _____?
    What factors were most important in you decision to
        _____?

3. *Verification*

    How did you feel after you decided to _____?

The sequence in which you ask these questions is not particularly important. But it is important to listen attentively to the answers.[2] These answers may be offered in direct response to your probing, or they may arise spontaneously in the course of your discussion.

Let's create an imaginary conversation to give you an idea of how you might determine another person's decision strategy. Imagine that you work for Jill Cramer, president of the Maxwell

Shipping Company. You'd like to convince Jill to install a new computer system (which would make your life much easier, because the present system is antiquated and inefficient). The conversation might go like this:

You: Jill, I've been trying to think of some ways we might speed up the flow of information. It's taking much too long for people to share necessary information because our computer system is antiquated.

Jill: Yeah, it has been a problem lately. But I really don't know what we can do right now. The cost of a new system is way out of our budget.

You: You may be right, Jill. Still, there must be something we can do. Of course we want to make sure to make the right decision and not spend money unnecessarily. The system we already have is still serviceable. I noticed though, that you replaced Hal's work station. Tell me, what caused you to decide to buy the Model XBZ? It has some interesting features.

Jill: Well, I talked to several different sales representatives. They came in and demonstrated their machines. And then I gave Georgia a call over at Acme Wiring. You know Georgia, she and I play golf on Sundays at the club. Anyway, Georgia said she'd looked at a whole bunch of machines and decided on the XBZ because the way they set up the financing on the thing it was cost-effective. Paid for itself in less than a year.

You: That's interesting. What got you interested in looking at new machines in the first place?

Jill: Well, it was Sarah over in Office Services. She got me thinking about it when she mentioned that Sam, that new guy they hired, had used a machine similar to the XBZ when he worked for

	Allied Air. He told her it saved them about $300 a month compared to the old machines they were using. Anyway, I got to thinking about it, and decided to call in the rep. Then I called around and had some other reps come over with their machines, and then I called Georgia, like I said before.
You:	And how did you feel after you decided to buy the XBZ?
Jill:	Well, I was a little worried. You know how sometimes those so-called time-saving wonder machines look great on paper, but when you actually try to use them they're more trouble than they're worth. But the salesman I bought it from said that he world have a service guy come over and spend as much time as we wanted going over the details with Hal, to make sure he understood how to use it.
You:	So it worked out OK?
Jill:	Yeah. The service guy only had to spend a couple of hours with Hal before he was using it like a pro.
You:	Jill, let me give some more thought to this matter of speeding up the flow of information around here and I'll get back to you in a couple of days.
Jill:	OK, you do that. But don't try to get me on Wednesday. I'm going to play some golf with Georgia.

If we were to analyze Jill's strategy for making this kind of decision, we would come up with something like this:

1. *Motivation.* Prompted to consider a new machine after Sarah told her of a possible savings.

2. *Decision.* Looked at a few alternatives, but relied most on Georgia's recommendation, which emphasized the financing available and the cost-effectiveness of the XBZ.

3. *Verification.* Had some doubts, but was reassured by the salesman, who promised, and delivered, adequate service support.

Notice that Jill is greatly influenced by other people, needs a few alternatives, and is convinced by cost-effectiveness. She has some second thoughts (buyer's remorse) after coming to a decision, but is reassured by the promise and delivery of good service. You now have enough information to design a presentation strategy to persuade Jill to invest in a new computer system.

How to Present Your Ideas in Virtually Irresistible Ways

When you have identified another person's decision strategy for a certain kind of decision, you have the tools essential for the power of persuasion. If the decision-maker has made this kind of decision before, he or she has probably evolved a pattern.

The essential pieces of this pattern are present in the strategy you elicited. If you have any doubts about the pattern, find out how he or she made other decisions of the same kind and pick out the recurring themes. It doesn't make a lot of difference whether the strategy you elicit is precisely accurate—as a matter of fact it most likely won't be. We all delete in our representations of our experience, and we also delete in the telling of our experiences.

The task now is to use the pattern you elicited in putting together your presentation. The development of a presentation strategy is simply a translation of the decision strategy, and it looks like this:

Decision Strategy	Presentation Strategy
Motivation	Interest
Decision	Conviction
Verification	Reassurance

In other words, when you know how a person is typically motivated to engage in decision making, you will know how to get him or her interested in considering your idea. When you know how he or she makes the actual decision, you will know how to convince him or her to accept your idea. And when you know how the person verifies the decision, then you will know how to reassure him or her, if necessary. In Jill's case, your job now is to interest her in a new computer system, convince her that it's a good idea, and finally, reassure her that she's made the right decision when she agrees to buy it.

Because Jill is motivated by other people (third-party influence), it might be a good idea to talk with Sarah and some of the other people over in Office Services to find out their thoughts on getting a new computer system. Given Jill's pattern, if you don't have the agreement and support of Sarah and her staff, it's unlikely that Jill will show much interest. You'll also want to find out what Sarah knows and thinks about the cost-effectiveness of a new system compared with the machines now being used. In addition, you'll want to talk with several sales representatives about cost-effectiveness, financing, and support service. It would also be a good idea to find out if Georgia (or some other good friend of Jill's) has installed a new computer system lately. A recommendation from somebody Jill knows and respects would probably be the clincher.

Here's how you might map out your presentation strategy for Jill:

Interest. Tell Jill you have checked with Sarah, some of her staff, and have also talked with several sales representatives of computer systems. You've come up with what you think might be a cost-effective way to speed up the flow of communication, and you'd like her opinion.

Conviction. In this stage, you might ask Sarah to come in and give Jill her ideas about computer systems and the possible savings advantages. It would also be a good idea to have a few of the sales representatives you've talked with come in to demonstrate their products. (Make certain that you've discussed the financing of their various products and have weeded out the programs that don't meet what you know will be Jill's specifications.) If you've been able to locate a business associate or friend of Jill's who has had good success with computer systems, be sure to mention it to Jill and suggest she give this person a call. Finally, make sure you are familiar with the service support offered by each of the computer system manufacturers, and brief the salespeople on how important this is to Jill.

Reassurance. After Jill has given her OK to install a new system, be sure to reassure her about the service support. You might even volunteer to supervise this activity, to guarantee that all goes smoothly.

If you do all these things, you should be able to present your idea to Jill in a way that is virtually irresistible. Keep in mind that people do things for their reasons, not for yours. The art of persuasion consists of being able to determine what those reasons are and then presenting your ideas in ways that fit the habitual decision processes of the people you want to influence.

The process you just went through with Jill is a simplified version of what can sometimes be a much more comprehensive and lengthy process. For example, in identifying and using another person's decision strategy you might need to consider the following:

Dominant perceptual mode. Is the other person primarily interested in the visual aspects (how it looks), or auditory (how it sounds, what others will say, whether the idea answers the questions he or she has been asking), or the feeling (how comfortable the person feels with the idea)?

Amount of information needed to make the decision. Some people require exhaustive amounts of information; others require very little.

Number of alternatives. Some people seem to need to consider every possible alternative; others need only one or a very few.

Third-party endorsements. Some people will decide only if a credible third party or parties recommend a particular course of action.

Amount of time required to reach a decision. If a person typically takes a long time to make a decision, you can't expect him or her to feel comfortable in acting quickly on your proposal. If fast action is required, then do all you can to help the person gather as much of the information that he or she will want. Do as much of the legwork as you can, and control as much as possible the time and manner in which this information is given to your prospect. Also keep in mind that if a person has a decision strategy that requires too much information or too much time, you have your work cut out for you. If you have a choice you may want to exercise it prudently by deciding to spend your time and energy persuading someone else.

If you follow all of these guidelines, and you have a good idea (one in which the benefits to the other person outweigh the disadvantages), then your presentation should be almost irresistible.

In most instances, similar themes run through all of a person's decision strategies. However, the state of a person's finances, prevailing economic conditions, the availability of information and alternatives, and the context within which the decision must be made all affect the decision process. A person's strategy also depends on the nature of the decision to be made. If for instance, this is the first time he or she has bought an automobile or a home, the decision strategy might be somewhat different from that used for buying an accustomed service or product. Also, a person might buy a car for personal use somewhat differently from the way he or she buys one for business use. In addition, decision-making strategies usually change over time. As a person becomes accustomed to making a certain kind of decision, he or she will simplify the process. Making decision after decision of a particular kind streamlines the decision strategy.

The important thing to keep in mind is that once a pattern for a particular kind of decision has been established, that overall pattern or strategy becomes difficult to change and consequently, easy to predict. It is, therefore, to your advantage to find out how the other person made a previous decision similar to the one you want to influence. Then tailor your presentation to fit the set pattern.[3]

Over the years I've had an opportunity to work with thousands of individuals in various workshops and seminars. One of the most frequent responses regarding decision strategies is surprise—people are surprised at how patterned and predictable their strategies are. Maybe everyone wants to believe that he or she is spontaneous and unpredictable, free from the confines of mundane habit.

The truth is people are not that spontaneous—at least with regard to those behaviors needed to be functional in life—and forming habitual ways of doing things is a survival mechanism. If we had to think and plot out all our various behaviors every time we did something we'd soon get bogged down in minutiae. It's both efficient and effective to have predictable patterns of behavior. And it's extremely important to recognize others' patterns in order to interact effectively with them.

I recall a seminar I did a few years ago for a group of research chemists. The subject of the seminar was how to work with people who have ways of processing information that are different from our own. One of the participants was a chemist whom I'll call 'Lee.' When we reached the part of the seminar having to do with identifying and using other people's decision strategies decisions I could see that Lee was getting increasingly uncomfortable. So I asked him what was going on.

"What's the matter, Lee?" I said.

"Well," he replied, "My boss and I have been working on a presentation for the vice president of marketing of one of our divisions. The purpose of the presentation is to sell the idea of investing a substantial sum of money to develop a particular product, and this vice president is the guy who can approve the expenditure.

"So what's the problem?" I asked.

"This whole discussion is convincing me that the presentation my boss and I have been working on is totally wrong for the vice president."

"In what way?" I asked.

"Well," Lee went on, "the presentation we've been working on is very technical and explains in detail how we're proposing to make the product. My manager and I know exactly what we're talking about, but the vice president of marketing isn't a chemist and isn't even very technically inclined. All he wants to know is whether this product will place us in a competitive place in the marketplace and be a profitable addition to the product mix. In other words, all he's really interested in is the bottom line."

"That's a good observation," I said. "What are you going to do about it?"

"We're going to have to completely redo the presentation and emphasize the bottom line and put all the detail discussion in an appendix that will assure him that we've done our homework and know what we're talking about. He won't have to wade through it to try to understand. We'll put the bottom line implications up front and use language that he can easily understand and relate to."

I checked back with Lee a few days later to find out how the presentation had gone.

"It went really well," Lee told me. "The vice president said at the end he liked our idea and said that it was the first presentation by a chemist that had ever made much sense to him."

"That's great," I said. "And how did your boss feel about revising the presentation."

"Well, when I first told him we needed to make these changes he was pretty upset. It was really important to him that we tell the story of how we'd developed this process, how it was unique technically, and so forth. But I was able to convince him that we could still put all that into the presentation, only we'd put it in an appendix for the vice president to review later on. My boss wasn't sure this new approach would work, but we'd made presentations to this particular vice president before without much success, so he was willing to try something different. And after the presentation he was really delighted that the vice president was so pleased with our idea. He shook his head a couple of times, though, and said he still couldn't quite believe that anyone would sign off on a program like the one we were proposing without thoroughly understanding how the product is made. I told him we could always go into that later, if anybody in marketing wanted to know."

The moral of the story is pace the other person's various processes and you'll be able to lead him or her much more effectively and much more successfully.

Identifying Decision Strategies: A Variation on the Theme

Getting information about previous decisions and extrapolating the strategies from them is an excellent idea. Sometimes, though, in the real world you don't have the opportunity or the time to do this kind of elicitation. You have to go with what you have.

For example, two clients had interestingly complementary decision strategies. Gary was a highly analytical sort who made his decisions based on the implications of the decision for virtually everyone involved in the decision. His partner, Grace, had a very different style. She saw very clearly what she wanted ("in living, vivid, moving picture color," as she described it).

During the early years of their partnership Grace couldn't understand why it took Gary so long to make a decision. She couldn't understand why anyone could take so long to figure out what he wanted. She assumed that everyone knew exactly what he or she wanted and that the only thing that remained was to figure out exactly how to get it. She thought that Gary's decision style was really a pretext designed to cloak his ulterior motives, which had to do with manipulating others to come around to his way of seeing things.

Over the years, Grace came to realize that her ability to know exactly what she wanted was a rare thing, a gift that not everyone possessed. Other people had different, perhaps less efficient, but no less legitimate, ways of arriving at conclusions that were for her immediately clear.

The best way to present an idea to Grace was to position it such that it supported, or dovetailed with her vision. She could be convinced that her initial decision was not the best alternative, but it was difficult and one had to use forceful logic to sway her.

Gary, on the other hand, did not have many pre-conceived ideas about what should be done in any given situation. He generally was motivated to consider a decision by an idea or suggestion someone else brought to him or by some feeling he had that something needed to be done about a particular issue.

He would invite discussion and delighted in constructing very complex problem statements that took into consideration the implications of all the various alternatives for all the various stakeholders. Understandably, his process often drove Grace to distraction. Fortunately, however, since he was open to many difficult alternatives, if Grace had a strong predilection for a particular course of action and if the implications for others were relatively benign, Gary would usually go along with her vision.

When Gary and Grace understood their respective decision strategies and had learned to communicate those strategies to their employees, they were in a much better position to get what they wanted. Before that, many of their employees had been confused about how to present ideas to them. Most of their employees knew that they were different but no one had sat down with each of them to map out the differences and to plot the best presentation strategies to use for each of them.

The chart below is a very simple yet very powerful tool that will assist anyone who works with Gary and Grace to do so more effectively. You can construct a similar chart for anyone you work with by asking the kinds of questions posed above. Sometimes you can get all the information you need from the individuals themselves; sometimes you'll have to ask other people who work with or for them. When you do this, it's a good idea to seek out individuals who have been successful working with the people you want to influence.

Together, Gary and Grace devised the following:

Decision Strategy	Presentation Strategy
Grace Has very clear vision of desired outcome, moving pictures, in vivid color. Can be convinced by strong logic.	Know what her vision is with respect to the particular area in which you want a decision. Present your ideas in ways that dovetail with her vision or help support it. If your idea conflicts with her vision, present your case logically and forcefully (but don't expect to convince her easily; keep relating your ideas to ways they support or enhance her vision, if not immediately, then ultimately).
Gary Usually doesn't have preconceived outcome. Constructs complex problem statement with many variables. Considers implications of an idea for all relevant stakeholders.	Introduce the idea as something you have a strong feeling about. Explore with him the implications of your idea(s) for the relevant stakeholders (but make sure you've done this in advance to test the merits of your idea)

Challenging the Process

A nother variation on this theme of identifying and using decision strategies to influence others is given by Kathleen Burke, currently the Executive Director of the Stupski Family Foundation in Tiburon, California. Kathi is an attorney and was Executive Vice President at Security Pacific Bank from 1978 to 1992, became their Corporate Secretary in 1988, and then the head of Human Resources in 1989. When Bank of America acquired Security Pacific in 1992, Kathi came in as Group Executive Vice President of Human Resources. During her tenure, she was promoted to Vice Chairman, the highest level to which any woman had ever risen at B of A.

I talked with Kathi about her experiences and the strategies she used to achieve her remarkable success. One of the tasks she undertook—first at Security Pacific and later at Bank of America—was to challenge the ways in which both banks treated woman and people of color.

JR: What did you observe at Security Pacific, and then later at Bank of America, that caused you to challenge the process?

KB: During my early years at Security Pacific, I never felt any personal discrimination. I did, however, observe attitudes and behaviors among the male senior managers, as well as the lack of women in senior roles, that caused me to be pessimistic about women's chances for advancement to the policy-making level.

So when they let me in the door at the top policy level, it was my license to challenge them on some of their practices and ways of doing business that made the environment more difficult for woman and people of color to succeed. I was very energized by that and also appreciative of the fine line I had to walk. I saw more aggressively outspoken women challenge things openly and I saw the curtain come down, and I didn't want that to happen. So I tried to be more effective about the way I challenged.

JR: How were you different in the way you challenged the process?

KB: I had a good understanding of the business and I appreciated what people were trying to accomplish, but I perceived a problem with the manner in which they were trying to accomplish it with groups of people who did not look like them and did not aspire to be like them. I believed that they would have to think about other ways of relating to different people and other ways of listening to them if they wanted to optimize their effectiveness. I kept relating everything to the business and tried to get them to see how they were missing opportunities to enhance people's productivity by the way they behaved.

JR: It sounds like you put your challenge into a frame of reference of how they could be more effective rather than how they were wrong, which is the way a militant critic will sometimes issue a challenge.

KB: Right. I also saw that many women and people of color didn't get the kind of good, critical, straightforward feedback they should have gotten along the way from their superiors. Consequently, they weren't doing things in a manner that would position them for a promotion or a transfer. And their male colleagues, by and large, had a better shot at getting that kind of feedback, so they could course-correct and present themselves as likely candidates when an opportunity came up. So a lot of women and people of color didn't know what to attribute their lack of success to other than gender or race. And I can appreciate why they felt that way. But I believed there was a way to address that without saying, "You guys are discriminating" or "Look at the numbers, you must be doing things wrong."

I believed that the managers owed everybody an equal chance even though it was only natural for them to feel less comfortable giving that kind of feedback—but they had to give feedback to everyone and I knew we could help them do it. They had to talk turkey with the people who were different from them, and if they couldn't articulate that feedback then maybe there was a problem. I tried not to be blameful, but I said, "I see a problem here and here's my perception of what's at the root of it. I think we can get at it and have a much more productive workplace, as well as avoid lawsuits and all that other stuff that is important but doesn't really change the way people act."

From an NLP perspective what Kathi did—which is a tactic often used by individuals effective in the art of persuasion—was to adopt what is referred to as "second position,"[4] which is the ability to see things from the other person's point of view. She goes on to describe her experiences later at B of A:

KB: I had an interesting experience when I joined Bank of America. I had a conversation with CEO Richard Rosenberg about Rosabeth Moss Kanter's rating of companies on a scale of 1 to 5, with 1 being the company doesn't even think there's an issue to 5 where everybody is treated like an individual and there aren't any gender or race issues. He asked me where I thought B of A was. At this point I'd been with the company for a couple of months and in the transition period for another five or six months. I told him I thought B of A was a 2 aspiring to be a 3, which he really didn't want to hear. I told him why I thought that and that I'd like to get the bank to at least a 3 if not to a 4.

He agreed with my thinking and said, "Would you be the after dinner speaker at our upcoming management strategic planning meeting and talk to people about this issue?" At that time it was one other woman and I and about 35 men who were running the company. So I agreed to do it because I thought this was something I ought to do.

Since I didn't yet understand the culture as well as I understood the Security Pacific culture, I invited a group of women over to my house one night for pizza. And I said to them, "I'm going to be standing up in front of your bosses talking about this issue and I want to be better informed about the environment that you see and the issues that you see." Well, it became very clear that these women did not trust me, they didn't trust one another and they weren't about to talk about any of this in a group. They were scared that I was going to screw up and it was going to run down hill. They wanted to know if Dick Rosenberg knew I was having this meeting.

I remember tossing and turning that night thinking, "My God, this is really a problem." And then the next day I got a phone call from one of my male direct reports saying that the rumors were rampant that I had held a clandestine radical feminist meeting at my house and what the hell was I doing, we didn't do things like that at B of A.

And then one of my colleagues on the policy committee came storming into my office and said that the guy next to him on the Stairmaster at the gym that morning had told him about this meeting and what the hell was I up to? And I said to myself, "This company has a problem."

So I used that story in my remarks. Fortunately it went well. I used statistics and I laid it all out and I said, "This company has got to break the code of silence around this issue." And it ended up being a very productive session. The next morning the CFO was supposed to kick off the meeting with a financial discussion but he said, "You know, I want to revisit some of the stuff we talked about last night because that's more important." So what started out looking like a huge disaster because it was a door nobody wanted to open turned out instead to be a huge success.

JR: So it sounds to me as though one of the things you do very well is to understand other people's points of view, how they think, and then couch your argument, your position, your point of view in terms they can understand, using the same standards of measurement that they use.

KB: Yes, that's one of the keys. I also think about who's going to be affected by this decision and what are they protective about—not necessarily about a particular decision but generally speaking. And I think, "How much time do I have to make this decision? Is this something I have to do right now, is it an emergency, or is it something I have a week to think about, or until the next board meeting? And I try to count backward—I do try to think about how many people are going to care about this decision, and at least try to tap into some representatives to get their perspective on it. I can usually craft a better decision because I'll have more data. But if I don't have time I don't do this, I take my best shot based on what I know at the time. But I like to have the time to get some input because in an organization everybody's going to have a point of view and you never know who's going to sabotage you.

I also was a very astute student of anybody who had to approve my decision before I could implement it, and I used the same format for my argument that I knew they used for their other business decisions. I learned that from my experience as Corporate Secretary at Security Pacific. I'd sit in board meetings and observe those executives who successfully negotiated that decision-making process and those who did not. I learned how to present information and anticipate the questions board members were likely to ask, and I learned that you might as well deal with those questions up front.

But I was never going after consensus, because in a large organization you'll never get it. I made some pretty big changes to the HR department which were not popular with some people, both within the HR department and with individual clients within the company. But I was convinced they made good business sense and I was able to convince the people who did need to agree and help implement, and then all I had to worry about was the communications issue to get everybody else on board. But I was able to get the right decision-makers on board for the big controversial changes.

From an NLP perspective what's most relevant from this interview is Kathi's conscious modeling of behaviors she saw to be successful and the incorporation into her presentations of the decision styles and formats used by others who had been successful. Although she might not have been aware of it at the time, Kathi successfully used many of the patterns of persuasion employed (often unconsciously) by many of the world's greatest communicators. And even though Kathi didn't use the exact model described earlier in this chapter to elicit the decision strategies of each of the individuals she would be presenting to, it's apparent that her method was to obtain as much information as possible about the people who would be evaluating her various proposals and to present her ideas in ways that to them would be virtually irresistible.

Modeling Other People

One of the most useful aspects of NLP is its emphasis on modeling other people who are able to do things that you want to be able to do. It's a relatively simple concept and can be conceptualized very easily. My first introduction to the idea came from one of my first employers. The first day on the job I went up to him and said, "Boss, here I am. What do you want me to do?" "Jerry," he replied, motioning to the work floor area, "I want you to go out there and find somebody who's working and imitate 'em."

That's still among the most profound pieces of advice I've received on the subject of learning to be successful. Find somebody who's doing what you want to be able to do and imitate 'em.

One of most successful consultants I know is Patrick Bell, a San Francisco Bay Area management consultant who seems always to be booked. I asked him one day what the secret of his success is and he said that he had several, but that one of them was his 7 million dollar story.

"What's the 7 million dollar story?" I asked.

"The 7 million dollar story is what I tell prospects who ask me about the kind of work I do and what I might do for them. It goes like this:

> I had a client who wanted to sell his company, but it was in financial trouble. He was advised by his board of directors to get venture capital money. I told him he was crazy to do that. His problem wasn't undercapitalization; it was poor sales. He hated to sell and the results proved it! So I hired a recruiter to find a Vice President of Sales. The recruiter came up with two candidates and we flew them both out for interviews: One was a very smooth, elegant mature gentleman with beautifully quaffed silver hair, who looked and acted very much like my client. The other was a squat little guy who was aggressive and abrasive. After we'd talked with both of them, my client said, "I really like Jim" (the mature gentleman). "That's why you're going to hire Lenny," I told him.
>
> "Why?!?" he said. "I didn't like him at all. He's a horrible person!"
>
> "You're going to hire him because Jim is too much like you and you hate selling. That horrible Lenny is going to make you a lot of money," I said.
>
> And he did. Two and a half years later my client sold the company for 7 million dollars.

Patrick's story is very useful for anyone looking for a good model of how to tell a persuasive story. In NLP this is often referred to as using metaphor. In this context a metaphor is usually a story that parallels (paces) the situation of the person to whom you're telling the story, with the implication (the lead) being that the listener should heed the moral of the story. All good salespeople tell stories to get their points across, and the more nearly the elements in the story match the elements in the listener's experience the more powerfully persuasive the story is likely to be.

In the story above, Patrick is telling his prospect that one of the most valuable things he does is to penetrate the prospect's blind spots and to get him (or her) to do things that he (or she) might not otherwise do, but that could very well save the farm. Patrick doesn't say that directly, and it's possible that many prospective clients wouldn't make the conscious connection, but the message is very clear to the unconscious mind. And because he's speaking to the unconscious mind, the story is even more powerful because it's operating at a level less subject to resistance.

Another excellent model of success is Patrick Connolly, the CEO of Myevents.com. This is Patrick's third successful Internet startup company. One of his previous ventures is now in the top 3% of all Internet companies with respect to revenues generated. I asked him one day where he learned to do the things necessary to create, run and sell a successful company.

"Not in college," he replied. "I just picked it up from different people. I've always admired people who can learn and adapt through imitation. I do it all the time. I look at someone and I think, 'The way that person interacts and treats other people, that's really cool. I should try to do that.' You watch and learn how people operate, how their patterns work and their brains function. So consciously I make a decision to emulate what they're doing—not imitation exactly but adaptation of their patterns. My friend Dan taught me how to be a good businessman. You can take pieces from different people and assimilate them. It's not like you don't have a personality. Your personality becomes what goes on around you, and that's good."

Patrick's strategy for excellence is based on the principle of modeling in others those qualities you want to incorporate in yourself. We all do it. To a large extent it's what we've done to become who we are. In most cases our models were our parents, our teachers, the athletes we admire, entertainers, prominent public figures, and others who have impressed or inspired us. What NLP does is to provide guidance about how to make certain kinds of behavioral distinctions that are not apparent to most people.

We've looked at some of these distinctions, such as behavioral pacing and leading, identifying and using others' perceptual biases (representational systems), and decision strategies. The rest of this book will discuss additional strategies that you can use to increase your personal power in any situation.

Future-Pacing

Pacing is something you do in the present moment to get into alignment with another person. Future-pacing (a term coined by Bandler and Grinder) enables you to exercise control over something that might happen in the future. Future-pacing is anticipating problems that may arise, or objections that the other person may raise, and providing for their solution in advance. For example, if you think the other person might later regret his or her decision, you may want to future-pace his or her behavior and allay his or her fears in the following way:

> In my experience, John, many people have questions that arise naturally later on. If any questions come up for you, what I'd like you to do is reach for the phone (here you could even simulate reaching for the phone) and give me a call. I'll be glad to do whatever needs to be done.

The important point here is that you will want to make certain to future-pace the other person's behavior. Then, when he feels remorse, he will call you to reassure him rather than to cancel the decision.

Anchoring: A Powerful Unconscious Resource

One of the most controversial techniques developed by Bandler and Grinder is *anchoring*. Anchoring is a method for using the powerful unconscious resources of others to get the responses you desire. It is the process by which a memory, a feeling or some other response is associated with (anchored to) something else. Anchoring is a natural process that usually occurs without our being aware of it. For example, when you were young you no doubt participated in family activities that gave you great pleasure. The pleasure was associated with the activity itself, so that when you think of the activity or are reminded of it you tend to re-experience some pleasurable feelings. In this way, anchors are reactivated, or triggered. For example,

- Thumbing through a family picture album stirs pleasant memories and some of the feelings associated with them.
- An old love song reawakens a romantic mood.
- The smell of freshly baked apple pie brings back a happy, carefree childhood memory.
- A gesture by a stranger reminds you of one your father used to make when he was angry, and you experience a momentary panic.
- A recurring theme in a musical composition carries with it the emotional overtones from the scene in which it was first introduced.

Most of the time, we are not aware that our responses are being anchored to these "triggers." This makes anchoring a powerful force in our lives. It is so powerful because it is invisible.

You can trigger anchors in yourself by using a technique advocated by drama teacher Uta Hagen:

> To bring about tears, the beginning actor's tendency is to think sad things, to pump for that mood or that general state of being, to try to remember a sad occasion, the story of that occasion, and then pray to God that somehow he will be catapulted into an appropriate emotional response somewhere along the way. I used to make all of these mistakes and could never understand why once in a while, somewhere along the line, something did indeed happen to me. But I must emphasize that it happened only once in a while, not inevitably, and it usually took a long time before it occurred. Sometimes I managed to work myself into a near trauma offstage, which brought me on with the sensation of moving in glue. After a few years, I discovered intuitively that what sent me correctly was a tiny remembered object only indirectly connected with the sad event: a polka-dot tie, an ivy leaf on a stucco wall, a smell or sound of sizzling bacon, a grease spot on the upholstery, things as seemingly illogical as those.[5]
>
> To experience for yourself what I am speaking about, tell a friend the story of an unhappy event in your life: tell him, for example, about a time when your lover walked out on you, blaming you unjustly for infidelity. Now tell your friend what surrounded the event; describe everything you can remember about the weather, the pattern of the drapes, a branch brushing against the window, the rumpled collar of your lover's shirt, the smell of the after-shave he was wearing, a frayed corner of the carpet, the tune that was playing on the radio as he left, etc., etc., etc. One of these objects will suddenly release the pain anew and you will weep again.[6]

Anchoring is also used by skillful film-makers to evoke suspense in the audience. Remember the movie *Jaws*? Think of your own psychological changes that occurred when you heard the soundtrack's amplified, pounding heartbeat rhythm in the moments leading up to each of the appearances of the huge killer shark. What anchor was established in you by the crescendo of the sound of the music meeting the sight of the shark? Did you begin to squirm? Did your heartbeat increase? Palms begin to sweat? Did you have to see the shark, or was the thumping music enough to start your slide to the edge of your seat?

This same anchoring process appears naturally and spontaneously in our dealings with others, and often determines the outcome of these interactions.

Before taking a client to see a home, California real estate dealer Gael Himmah always visits the property owners for the purpose of discovering the "emotional appeal" their homes particularly hold for them. Who else could better know? "What," he asks, "do you like best about your home? What features mean the most to you?"[7] One answer, given in an especially run-down house, led to an incident that reveals the potent effects of emotional recollections.

His question to the woman of the house led to a trip into the kitchen where she pointed proudly out the window towards a colorless, run-down garage. "In the springtime," she explained, "I plant sweet peas in that bed. There's something in the soil, and the temperature against the side of the garage, we're not sure what causes it, but the sweet peas grow all over the side of the garage and onto the roof and they're the biggest sweet peas anyone has ever seen. People come from all over to look at our sweet peas."[8]

Himmah now had his emotional feature neatly tucked away, and before too long he had the house sold to another couple. Some time later, he returned to find out from the new owners just what had prompted them to buy. In this case, however, he was not prepared for the husband's angry answer.

"Do you know what you've done to me?" he asked, his voice seething with menace.

"I just wondered how you like your new home?" I countered.

He wasn't having any. "Do you know what you've done to me?" he repeated.

"Not really," I said. It was a totally honest statement. I didn't have the slightest idea what he was talking about. Buyers can get strange.

"You and your damn sweet peas," he exploded. "That's all my wife could talk about after you showed us this house. Those damn sweet peas. When she was a little girl in New Jersey, she and her mother used to plant sweet peas and Iceland poppies every year. They took care of them together. She hadn't seen sweet peas since we moved to California ten years ago.

"This spring," he went on, fire in his eyes, "I'm going to have to send an airline ticket to my mother-in-law in New Jersey and she's flying out here and she and my wife are going to plant those damn sweet peas and she's going to stay all summer with us to watch them grow."

By this time he was breathless, the thought of his mother-in-law's prolonged visit working him into a rage.[9]

Anchoring needn't, of course, create domestic discord. But it is a very powerful resource and should be used wisely.

How to Anchor

When you're with another person who experiences some strong emotion, whatever you're doing or saying at that point in time becomes associated with that emotion. Usually this process occurs at the unconscious level. Subsequently, whenever you do or say the same thing in the same way in the presence of that person you will tend to restimulate for him or her some portion of the previous feeling.

Being aware of this phenomenon enables you to pay attention to the kinds of responses you are anchoring in others, how you're doing it, and conversely, what kinds of responses are being anchored in you by others (whether consciously or not) and how. This awareness enables you to anchor for mutually productive outcomes.

For example, let's say a father and his young son are having a discussion. The son is emotionally distraught, sobbing deeply. In a well-intentioned attempt to comfort him, the father reaches out and touches his son's arm. This act could have a powerful impact in either of two ways. First, if the father had previously established this anchor while his son was in a positive emotional state, the act of touching should serve to trigger the positive anchor and elicit the desired response (or some part of it). But if the father had not previously established this anchor, he might unintentionally be anchoring his son's sobbing, distraught state. The effect of this might be that the next time he touches him on the arm, he could awaken the undesired state of emotional distress.

This example provides at least a partial explanation for the unpleasant feelings we sometimes experience when we are physically touched by someone who is otherwise close to us. It also suggests that we need to be particularly aware of the patterns and precedents we set in our relations with other people. If, in fact, we touch another person only when he or she is emotionally upset, we may inadvertently be conditioning that person to feel upset whenever we do touch him or her.

In general, then, it would seem to be a wise policy to establish physical contact with another person when he or she is feeling good about something. This way, when the other person is in distress, your touch will tend to restimulate those good feelings, thereby providing genuinely helpful emotional support.

How to Elicit the Responses You Want

The process of eliciting and re-eliciting desired responses from bosses, clients, friends, or spouses is a fairly simple one. Ask the person involved to recall a past experience that is likely to contain the desired response. For example, if you want the individual to experience a pleasurable response ask him or her to recall a pleasant incident. In doing so, the person will bring up, with that memory, many of the feelings felt at the time of the incident.

The purpose of eliciting certain responses is to establish a more favorable and receptive ground for communicating your ideas effectively. The person's state of mind, his or her feelings, the things he or she is attending to (both consciously and unconsciously), will be of critical significance with regard to how he or she receives your ideas and suggestions. By eliciting the kinds of responses you want when you present your idea, you increase the chances of having your idea favorably received and acted on. This will come as no surprise to anyone who has ever tried to sell anything, but even the most sophisticated salesperson often ignores this basic fact.

Imagine for a moment that you represent a manufacturer of golf equipment. You have a line of golf clubs that you know would be ideally suited for you prospect, George Downs. During your visit with George, you might ask him to tell you of one of his most pleasant recent experiences on the links. As he recounts the experience, it is inevitable that some of the excitement and pleasure of the original experience will be reactivated.

How to Anchor Specific Responses

When George's reactivated excitement reaches its peak, if you do something that he can detect (even at the unconscious level), you will at that moment connect his response to a specific behavior of yours. In addition, you can re-elicit the same response (or some part of it) at some future moment by again performing the same action.

Here's an example of how this works. Suppose George is describing that very long golf drive off the fourth tee. As he speaks, his eyes light up, his breathing rate increases, and his speech and mannerisms become more animated. In short, he is excited.

What you can do when the excitement reaches its peak is to lean forward, touch him on the arm, and say, "That really must have given you a *good* feeling," with particular emphasis on the word "good." What you have accomplished in doing this is to anchor George's feeling of excitement to a particular set of behaviors on your part—in this case, leaning forward, touching him on the arm, and saying "good." The effect is to store in George's unconscious mind the feeling of excitement, coupled with your particular behavior at the moment of that excitement. You have thus created a new memory in his mind, one that you can reactivate whenever you choose.

After anchoring George's excitement associated with the golf drive, suppose you want to ensure that he will be maximally receptive to your suggestion about purchasing that set of golf clubs. You might say, "George, from what you've told me about your game and the needs you have right now (leaning forward and touching his arm), I think you'll find these clubs to be a *good* (same intonation) investment in your game. How do you feel about that?"

If you properly anchored George's earlier response, the feeling he will be experiencing now should bear a close resemblance to the previous feeling of excitement that he experienced when he first described his long golf drive. This will make it much easier for George to anticipate some of the pleasure he will get when he uses the clubs he's going to purchase from you. It will also make it much easier for you to complete the sale happily.

To summarize, the process of anchoring is accomplished in the following way:

1. Wait for the desired response to occur spontaneously or elicit the response by making appropriate suggestions or by asking such questions as

> What excites you about _____?
> What do you like about _____?
> Can you recall the last time you felt _____?

By asking the other person to recall a specific experience, some of the feelings associated with the memory will be reactivated and can then be anchored.

2. Anchor the response at its peak with some behavior of your own, such as one or more of the following:

> Verbal marking ("That's really a *fine* story!")
> A touch on the other person's arm
> A sound, such as snapping your fingers, or a particularly
>   expressive facial expression

3. Trigger the anchor at the desired moment by performing exactly the same action as in Step 2. (In the case of the verbal anchor, you might change the wording to "Let me tell you a really *fine* story!" In any case, the anchor here is primarily the word fine and should itself suffice as an anchor.)

Like any new skill, anchoring requires a certain amount of practice. Practice anchoring good feelings in your family, friends, and business associates. It will make both them and you feel good. It will also enable you eventually to do it unconsciously and appropriately to create a more receptive climate for your ideas and suggestions.

When you've learned to time your anchoring correctly, you should be able to anchor a response with only one attempt. In the meantime, just enjoy the pleasure of practicing a skill that will give you and the people you live and work with many happy hours. With experience, you will be able to effectively and appropriately anchor responses without even thinking about it, which is the ultimate goal.

An effectively established anchor will often last until some stronger emotional event intervenes to weaken the response. If this happens, simply re-establish the anchor in the same manner.

A Word of Caution

Anchoring is a very powerful process. Of all the techniques presented so far it offers, arguably, the greatest opportunities for misuse—manipulation in the negative sense of the word. Please be particularly careful when and how you use it. The objective is to heighten another's experience for positive purposes and mutually productive outcomes.

Embedded Suggestions

As the term implies, embedded suggestions are words and phrases enclosed (embedded) within a larger context. They are units of meaning that can often have an impact beyond that which is apparent in or intended by the larger structure within which they appear. For example, someone says to me, "I really feel bad today, Jerry." What is happening here goes beyond what is intended. The phrase, "feel bad today, Jerry," is an embedded suggestion to me to feel bad—even though the apparent reference is to the speaker, and not to me, the listener. If the speaker uses enough of these embedded suggestions, very soon I will very likely begin to respond to these suggestions, perhaps without even being consciously aware of doing so. For example,

This place is enough to *drive you crazy*.

I wish I had a nickel for every time that guy *gave me a hard time.*

Don't let me *keep you from working.*

And one of my all-time favorites, the triple whammy:

Don't *worry.* It's not *hard to find.* You can't *miss it.*

So pay attention to the embedded suggestions other people give you and avoid, insofar as possible, those toxic people who are—however unwittingly—casting a spell on you. If your work demands that you be around such people for extended periods of time, you can neutralize their effect on you by embedding positive suggestions of your own. For example, you might pace the other person by saying, "Yes, I know how you feel. I've felt that way before, too," and then lead with, "but I found that I could feel better, (name of other person), by making myself get out of here for a while."

Any word or phrase can be thought of as an embedded suggestion. The next time you turn on the radio or the television, pay attention to the words, phrases, and images used in the commercials. If the commercial has been skillfully constructed, the language used will be carefully crafted to produce a desired response. In this respect, embedded suggestions tug at the unconscious, awakening associations. These associations can inspire hope, fear, delight, anxiety, relief, tension, and so on. On the positive side, such words as *warm, soft, clean, powerful, bigger*, and *better*, when repeated in various combinations, have the cumulative effect of leading the listener to a particular state of mind, or set of experiences. Words such as *tight, tense, anxious, afraid, weak*, and *helpless* can cause you to have the feelings associated with the words.

Similarly, the words, phrases, and images you use in conversation also lead your listeners to a particular state of mind or set of experiences. The critical question is "Is it the result you want?"

Embedded Questions and Commands

Two types of embedded suggestions—questions and commands—deserve special attention.

An embedded question is an implied question that is embedded in a larger context, usually a statement. For example:

> I wonder *what your name is.*
> I'm curious to know *how old you are.*
> I don't know *what your income is.*"
> Whether *you'd like to come with me* is something we haven't discussed yet.

An embedded command is simply a command that is embedded in a larger context:

> I think *you'll be wise* if *you invest* in this property *today.*
> My mother used to tell me that the best way to *get over a cold* is to *stay in bed* and *get plenty of rest.*
> If anyone has any questions, I'd appreciate it if you'd *wait until after the lecture* and *come up to talk to me then.*

As you can see, we use embedded suggestions—both questions and commands—all the time. They're so pervasive as to be virtually invisible. Therein lies their power. This is a good reason for learning how to use them constructively and effectively.

Embedded questions and commands work so effectively because they are almost invisible. They operate for the most part at the unconscious level, and thus are not likely to cause resistance. People respond to the question or command below the level of awareness.

The cumulative effect is to gently lead the other person in the direction you want him or her to go. This phenomenon operates whether the other person is consciously paying attention to you or not. Embedding suggestions is an excellent approach to use with people who seem always too busy to give you their full attention.

Consider the boss who fiddles with paperwork when you're trying to get him to listen to an idea. Instead of being frustrated by his behavior, you might welcome it as an opportunity to embed suggestions. Because his mind is already distracted, you can easily continue talking while embedding appropriate suggestions that he will respond to unconsciously. The net effect will be to give him some "food for thought" to be digested unconsciously. Later on, you might be pleasantly surprised to hear him voicing your ideas as if he had thought of them himself or "spontaneously" acting on the suggestions you embedded earlier.

The tone of your voice and the emphasis you give the embedded suggestions are also very important. As you deliver the embedded suggestions, it's a good idea to tonally mark the parts you especially want the other person to respond to. As an example, let's listen in on a conversation between Sylvia, a stockbroker, and Ralph, her client. The italics indicate the tonally marked suggestions.

> Ralph: Sylvia, I know you're probably right about this investment, but I'm just not sure this is the time for me to be spending any more money.
>
> Sylvia: Ralph, I don't know whether *you're ready for such an investment*, but one thing I believe is that *people can make a lot of money, Ralph*, if they *invest in these stocks now.*

Additionally, by inserting Ralph's name next to the suggestion she wants him to attend to, Sylvia is further ensuring that he will respond to it. Our names are perhaps the most important words in our vocabularies. When we hear them mentioned, we listen more attentively.

Embedded suggestions will work wonders for you when you use them with the people in your life. They'll respond unconsciously, so that their resistance, at least at the conscious level, is avoided.

How to Control a Conversation

There are at least two useful observations to keep in mind when you're dealing with other people: (1) People like to talk more than they like to listen, and (2) the listener controls. The first idea hardly needs documentation. The second is a bit more elusive. The reason the listener controls is this: The listener is similar to the driver of a car. The speaker is like the engine, which provides the motive power, but the listener is at the wheel and provides the direction. By judiciously asking questions or making appropriate statements, the listener can guide the flow of conversation. Here's an example of how that can be done:

> Speaker: What we need to do is to get Charlie's group over in marketing to come up with a game plan for the Southwest.
> Listener: That's an interesting idea. Can you tell me how, specifically, that will generate more sales for the entire region?
> Speaker: Sure, first of all it will . . . (and so on).

The listener can also establish and maintain control of the flow of conversation by asking questions to clarify or redirect:

Does that mean _____?
What specifically do you mean by _____?

Or by paraphrasing:

What I understand you to say is _____. Is that right?

In addition to being an excellent active listening technique, paraphrasing has the effect of reinforcing the speaker, so that he or she continues to talk more. Another way to get a speaker to say more is to voice agreement. By verbally agreeing with a speaker, you are reinforcing him or her, thereby increasing the likelihood that he or she will continue talking.

If you want someone to stop talking, short of asking for quiet, there are at least two effective ways of winding down his or her urge to continue speaking: You can remain perfectly silent or you can disagree. Either of these will usually prompt the other person to seek companionship elsewhere.

Silence is the absence of any verbal feedback whatever. In behaviorist jargon, it is a form of "extinction," which is simply the refusal to reinforce a particular behavior. Extinction has been shown to be the most effective method for eliminating a behavior from a person's repertoire, even more effective than punishment (which, to be effective, must be administered with each instance of the undesirable behavior). This is why solitary confinement, the absence of any reinforcement or feedback from other humans, is even more feared than physical punishment.

One mistake many parents make when they want to quiet noisy children is to attempt to "punish" children for making noise, but often only succeed in reinforcing the very behavior they want to eliminate. Punitive attention, it seems, is preferable to none at all. So if you want someone else to be quiet, don't pay any attention to him or her, and he or she will eventually go away.

The other effective means for getting someone to go away and leave you alone is to disagree. This is the opposite of pacing and building rapport. Initially you might get an argumentative response, but if you maintain your contrariness long enough the other person will eventually go away and find someone else to talk with. It's important for us to find people who will validate our beliefs and opinions, and we all tend to "drop" people who disagree.

Silence and disagreement, of course, are rather drastic measures. Usually, simply telling the other person you've had enough for now will be sufficient. Still, it's useful to know there are other options if candor fails.

Summary

In this part of the book, we've examined how to get what you want in your dealings with others. The first rule is to know what you want and then ask for it. In addition, make sure that you ask in a way that makes sense to the other person. If you've paced the other person, you have an inner feeling about him or her, because you have established an empathic bond of rapport. In addition, emphasize the benefits to the other person of going along with your idea.

Identify and use the other person's decision strategy in order to design a presentation that is virtually irresistible. Anchor desirable responses during the course of your interactions with the other person, and then trigger those anchors appropriately to create an even more receptive climate for your ideas. Use embedded suggestions, questions, and commands to produce favorable responses and to avoid resistance at the unconscious level.

The listener controls the flow of the conversation by asking questions to redirect or clarify. By paraphrasing or agreeing with other people, you get them to talk more. By remaining silent or disagreeing with them, you terminate the discussion.

And finally, because of the power inherent in these techniques, use them wisely for mutually productive outcomes.

Suggestions for Practice

1. Practice asking for what you want. Regard rejections as a positive rather than a negative thing. It simply means you are getting closer to acceptance.

2. Identify the decision strategies of friends until the process becomes comfortable and natural for you. Then begin to identify the decision strategies of people you work with. Translate these decision strategies into presentation strategies when you want to persuade them to accept an idea. Notice how much easier it is to get your ideas accepted.

3. Anchor and then trigger pleasurable responses in the people you live and work with. Notice how much better both you and they feel when you're in each other's presence.

4. Pay attention to the embedded suggestions other people give you. This will help you identify your real friends.

5. Make a list of the words and phrases that suggest the kind of attitudes and feelings you'd like other people to have while being with you or while thinking about you. For example, "feel comfortable," "have a nice day," "have an open mind," "learn even more," "be even more productive," and "feel even more confident." Consciously embed these phrases in your conversations with others until you've developed the habit. Then notice how things and people begin to transform magically around and within you.

Part Three
Notes

[1] Jerry W. Koehler, Karl W.E. Anatol, and Ronald L. Applbaum, *Organizational Communication: Behavioral Perspectives* (New York: Holt, Rinehart and Winston, 1976), p. 219.

[2] There is a similarity here in this method of information gathering and the method sometimes referred to as *behavioral interviewing*. Behavioral interviewing is based on the empirically based observation that people are patterned in their behavior and that if you want to get a good idea of how people will behave in the future you can do so by finding out how they behaved in a similar situation in the past. A skilled behavioral interviewer will ask a job candidate, "Tell me about a time in the past when you had to discipline an employee. How did you do it?" This is a much more reliable type of questioning than is asking, "How do you discipline employees?" The former question will tell you how the candidate did it in the past; the latter will more likely tell you what the candidate thinks you want to hear.

[3] In *Sources of Power: How People Make Decisions*, consultant Gary Klein reports on research—his own and others'—in the field of Naturalistic Decision-Making, which has to do with how people make decisions in real-life situations, often under great pressure and where the stakes can be life and death. The conclusions he comes to are that professionals such as fire fighters, police officers, military personnel, et al., learn from extensive experience to make patterned decisions based on their assessments of frequently encountered situations. He calls this strategy *recognition-primed decision making*.

[4] First position is from your own point of view; second position is from the other person's point of view; third position is from an objective point of view.

[5] Uta Hagen, *Respect for Acting* (New York: Holt, Rinehart and Winston, 1976), p. 219.

[6] Hagen, p. 48.

[7] Gael Himmah, *Real Estate Selling Magic* (Gael Himmah

Publishing Co., 1974), p. 84.

[8] Himmah, p. 85.

[9] Himmah, p. 85-86.

PART FOUR

Dealing with Resistance

It's something you find everyday around the house.
—Groucho Marx

In this final part of the book, we're going to cover some approaches to dealing with other people's resistance to you and your ideas. We'll begin by exploring the nature of resistance and its causes. Then we'll examine in detail some specific kinds of resistance, such as resistance to change, reluctance by other people to open up to you, and objections. We'll discuss resistant personality types and what you can do to more effectively cope with them. The gentle art of reframing offers a technique that will enable you to get other people to see your point of view. Finally, we'll deal with anger and hostility and how to gracefully defuse it.

What It Is and How to Deal with It

A s a general rule, it's useful to regard another person's resistance as something you've created. This is so because the other person can only resist something you're doing or saying. Also, you have control only over your own behavior. So it's wise to regard resistance as your problem, not the other person's.

Another way of looking at this idea is that it is your resistance to the other person's resistance that causes the problem. Remove your own resistance, and you remove the problem. An effective way to change another's resistance into acceptance is to accept the other person's resistance. This may seem paradoxical, but it is only apparently so. The general principle is that when you're with another person, the resulting combination forms a system. When you change one part of the system (in this case, your behavior), you in fact change the whole system (which includes the other person's behavior).

If you've paced the other person effectively, you should encounter minimal resistance, if any. However, when you do encounter it, here is a suggestion that will apply in most instances: Change your behavior. Stop whatever it is you've been doing and do something else. (The temptation and tendency is to push harder with more of the same, which usually stiffens the other person's resistance.)

You might change your behavior by getting on the other person's side ("Agree with thine adversary quickly"). You can do this with integrity by getting into agreement with that part of the other person's position that you can legitimately agree with, even if it's only ten percent or involves a minor point. Look for and find an area of agreement. In so doing, you will have proved yourself an astute witness in the eyes of the other person. He or she will then be much more willing to listen to your side of the story (after all, you are both now on the same side). This approach may seem to lack logic, but in psychological affairs, the most important thing to most people is not to be logical, but to be right. Once you have accepted the other person and have acknowledged him or her to be right, you have, paradoxically, won the major battle. You're now both on the same side, and when this happens the resistance disappears. Frequently, you will be able to show the person your position without encountering further resistance. In other words, pace first, then lead.

Consider, for example, the following exchange between Atherton and Adrienne:

Adrienne: Atherton, I've been thinking it over, and I think we should implement that new procedure in the department. You know the one I'm talking about where we reorganize the work flow around the word-processing unit.

Atherton: No, I don't want to do that. We tried something like that a couple of years ago, and it didn't work. It didn't save any time at all. As a matter of fact, it caused such confusion that it took us almost twice as long to get anything done around here.

Adrienne at this point has to make a decision. She sincerely believes the new system will work and should be given a fair chance. She also believes she can prove that Atherton is wrong this time. However, she realizes that Atherton, like the rest of us, cherishes his beliefs and wants to be right.[1] So she decides to find an area of agreement. Atherton has told her, in so many words, that he thinks any new system should save time, not waste it. So she decides to use this point as the area of agreement:

> Adrienne: You know, Atherton, I think you're right. Any
> system we put in here has to save time.

With this reply, Adrienne has put herself on Atherton's side. So
she has made it safe to probe a bit to find out his reasons for
thinking this new system won't work. She knows that if he's
going to change his mind, it will be for his reasons, not hers.

> Adrienne: I'm sure you have some good reasons for
> believing this new system won't work. Would
> you mind telling me what they are?
> Atherton: Not at all. What happened during that last fiasco
> was that the genius who designed the
> system—some boy wonder from the Methods
> and Procedures department—didn't have the
> foggiest idea what we do around here. He
> thought we could just move a few desks around,
> change a couple of reporting assignments,
> implement a work-batching program, and
> everything would magically get done faster.
> Adrienne: And it didn't.
> Atherton: You bet your life it didn't. If he'd bothered to
> ask anybody around here why it wouldn't work,
> we could have told him. Why, I could have told
> him why it wouldn't work in a million years.

At this point, Adrienne is beginning to understand some of the
reasons for Atherton's resistance to the new system. Neither he
nor any of his department were asked to participate in designing
the system two years ago. Clearly, Atherton resented it then,
and resents now the possibility that the same thing could happen
again. Adrienne, now sensitive to this underlying issue, sees an
opportunity to lead the discussion into a more fruitful area:

> Adrienne: Atherton, what do you think we could do to make some improvements in the way the work flows in the department?
>
> Atherton: Oh, there's probably a lot of things we could do.
>
> Adrienne: What, specifically, would you suggest?
>
> Atherton: Well, the first thing I'd do would be to . . .

While Atherton is telling Adrienne what he'd do to solve the work flow problem, this might be a good time to examine some of the dynamics in the interaction that just took place. Adrienne realized she had restimulated an old wound for Atherton and had inadvertently triggered an anchor to a negative experience for him. So she quickly sought safe, common ground, an area of agreement, in sharing with him her concern for a system that was a time saver, not a time waster. She paced him, in other words. She then led him, by probing for more information. By getting into agreement, or alignment, with Atherton, she made it safe for him to open up to her. She was then able to get a better idea of his thinking on the issue, thereby enabling her to move into a problem-solving mode with Atherton. What if she had attempted immediately to counter his resistance with reasons why the new system should be implemented? There is little doubt that Atherton would have felt compelled to defend his position, thus tying up both his energy and hers in a fruitless win/lose affair. Instead, by aligning with him, Adrienne was able to redirect his energy in a more productive direction, that of seeking a solution to a problem that both of them would like to be rid of, namely the presently inefficient work flow arrangement. In all likelihood, Adrienne and Atherton will now be able to work together to design a system that will work. It will work because it will be a product of collaboration, not one handed down from above. The approach Adrienne took here leads to the next issue: resistance to change.

Resistance to Change

People do not resist change *per se*. What they resist is the uncertainty that accompanies the change. They especially resist the uncertainty surrounding their relationships with their fellow workers.

In the hypothetical interchange between Atherton and Adrienne, it became apparent that Atherton's resistance to the idea of a new system for improving the workflow was based on personal considerations not technical ones. Desks had to be moved around, and reporting assignments had to be changed. All this threatened the existing patterns of social relationships.

The way to deal with resistance to change is first to be aware of the dynamics, especially the established relationships that exist. Also, if possible, involve the individuals who are going to be affected by the change. Let them have a part in the analysis of the problem that the change is designed to solve. Let them participate in developing the solution. Adrienne plans to work with Atherton and his staff to solve the problem, so that they will share ownership in the solution. They will then put all of their energy into making the solution work rather than resisting somebody else's solution. And because they're closer to the problem than the people upstairs in the Methods and Procedures department, their approach to the problem will probably have the benefit of practical day-to-day experience—something that the people upstairs can't be expected to have.

In his classic article on this subject, Paul R. Lawrence has this to say:

> The key to the problem is to understand the true nature of resistance. Actually, what employees resist is usually not technical change but social change—the change in their human relationships that generally accompanies technical change. Resistance to methods changes (can) be overcome by getting the people

involved in the change to participate in making it. And participation is a feeling on the part of people, not just the mechanical act of being called in to take part in discussions.[2]

Lawrence goes on to say that staff people who are often given the task of analyzing and developing solutions for operations people to implement often focus so narrowly on the technical aspects of the problem that they fail to understand and appreciate the social relationships involved. "The staff man gets so engrossed in the technology of the change he is interested in promoting that he becomes wholly oblivious to different kinds of things that may be bothering people."[3]

Lawrence concludes by reminding us that social relationships at work make productivity possible:

> We must not forget that these same social arrangements which at times seem so bothersome are essential for the performance of work. Without a network of established social relationships, an organization would be populated with a collection of people who had no idea of how to work with one another in an organized fashion. By working with this network instead of against it, management's staff representatives can give new technological ideas a better chance of acceptance."[4]

This is the approach Adrienne has chosen to take with Atherton and his people. Together, they have a good chance of solving the problem.

Life Is Not a Contest

The best way to deal with resistance is to get into agreement, or alignment, with it, rather than to fight it. In many ways, this notion is foreign to Western cultural conditioning. As children (especially little boys), we were taught to be competitive. We played games that had winners and losers, and were told that the best thing is to be a winner and the worst thing is to be a loser. Boxing is perhaps the purest expression of this attitude. One man attempts to hammer another into submission, or, failing that, the outcome is decided by a panel of judges. The American legal system, in large part, is based on adversary relationships. The idea, and ideal, of competition and survival of the fittest permeates the thinking and ways of dealing with others in much of the Western world.

In contrast, the Eastern approach to life is based on cooperation and the harmonious resolution of conflict. Aikido, a relatively recently developed Japanese martial art, combines techniques from many older Eastern martial arts. It blends them into a subtle and sophisticated system for defending oneself while avoiding injury to the attacker. The idea is to align yourself with the attacker and to use his or her energy to foil the attack. You move with rather than against your opponent.

By using this approach, a small woman skilled in Aikido can easily throw a large man by using his energy, his momentum. Contrast this image with that of two fighters in the ring, each striving to batter the other against the ropes, and you have a picture of one of the essential differences between the Western and the Eastern approaches to dealing with resistance. In most instances the Eastern approach makes more sense and leads to more productive outcomes for all concerned.

This idea is also expressed by economist and management consultant Lester C. Thurow in *The Zero-Sum Society*:

> Our political and economic structure simply isn't able to cope with an economy that has a substantial zero-sum element. A zero-sum game is any game where the loses exactly equal the winnings. All sporting events are zero-sum games. For every winner, there is a loser, and winners can only exist if losers

exist. What the winning gambler wins, the losing gambler must lose.[5]

Life is not a contest. Sure, there are times when it's necessary to assume an adversarial posture. But the adversary role, playing a win/lose game, is best done as a last resort, not as the opening move. In general, whether at work or at home, resistance is best met with a win/win attitude. The question then becomes "How can we both win?" not "How can I make the other guy lose?" It becomes "How can we work together?" (as Adrienne is doing with Atherton and his staff), rather than "How can I prove that I'm right and he's wrong?" The win/lose, right/wrong game is a dangerous one to play, even when you win, or win the first round. As the worldly wise old baseball pitcher, Satchel Paige, put it: "Don't look back. Somethin' might be gainin' on you."

The benefits of a win/win attitude, however, are considerable. In negotiations, such an attitude can even increase one's power. R. G. H. Sui, in his fascinating (and delightfully Machiavellian) *The Craft of Power*, talks about the importance of this strategy:

> Objectives can often be more efficiently gained through accommodating than through mutually damaging [actions].
> One of the most esteemed persons of power during the 1930s in this regard was Sidney Hillman. He was leader of the Amalgamated Clothing Workers of America from its inception in 1914 to his death in 1946. Not only did he raise wages and improve working conditions for his union members, but also significantly influenced the president in national social policies. He was well known for his reasonableness even among the bargaining corporate executives. In 1934 the trade journal, *The Daily News Record*, wrote that "Mr. Hillman enjoys the confidence and respect of employers with whom he has dealt. It is generally said of him in employer circles that he has never made demands on an industry that it could not meet

economically and he has been known to make concessions where the realities of the situation proved irresistible."[6]

One of the benefits, then, of playing the game from a win/win position is that other people will continue to play with you, the effect of which is that you can continue to influence them. The most sensible strategy in attempting to deal with resistance and to resolve conflicts is to conspire to cooperate, whenever possible, rather than to compete. Even Machiavelli would agree. "Do good when you can," he said, "Do evil when you must." But if you do evil, be prepared for the consequences. Don't look back. Somethin' might be gainin' on you.

Getting Reluctant People to Open Up

Gaze for a moment at the dots below:

•   •   •

•   •   •   •

As you look, your mind immediately begins to see the dots on the left as three points of a triangle and the dots on the right as four points of a square.

Once it has become a part of your experience to see something in a certain (organized) way—in this case, a triangle or a square—it becomes difficult to see it in any other way. Your mind, in effect, refuses to view these dots as unconnected. What has once become whole, stays whole.

This insistence on seeing a triangle and square where none exists seems to be part of an overwhelming desire to discern an organized, meaningful whole. It is another way of bringing order to the world around us, like the language we use. As Wallace Stevens puts it in "The Idea of Order at Key West":

> And when she sang, the sea,
> Whatever self it had, became the self
> That was her song, for she was the maker. Then we,
> As we beheld her striding there alone,
> Knew that there never was a world for her
> Except the one she sang and, singing, made.
> Ramon Fernandez, tell me, if you know,
> Why, when the singing ended and we turned
> Toward the town, tell why the glassy lights,
> The lights in the fishing boats at anchor there,
> As the night descended, tilting in the air,
> Mastered the night and portioned out the sea,
> Fixing emblazoned zones and fiery poles,
> Arranging, deepening, enchanting night.
>   Oh! Blessed rage for order, pale Roman, The maker's rage to order words of the sea, Words of the fragrant portals, dimly-starred, And of ourselves and of our origins, In ghostlier demarcations, keener sounds.[7]

The urge to find order forms a distinct pattern of our behavior. In fact, a vague unease, an uncertainty, may well result from a failure to complete something that seems already started: Hearing the first three notes but not the accompanying fourth note of the beginning of Beethoven's Fifth Symphony, for example, or stepping onto an escalator that we suddenly realize isn't moving. Although the escalator forms a perfectly usable staircase, our expectation from past experience is such that we become momentarily uncoordinated, and our legs even wobble. It takes a few steps to reorient ourselves to the task of moving under our own power.

This disease, or frustration, caused by a failure to complete the expectation of something, to leave its potential unfulfilled, can be used to your advantage in dealing with others. Milton

Erickson gives an example of frustrating someone's speech as a way of encouraging the person to talk:

> Sometimes . . . I'll ask, "What is your name, how old are you, what town did you come from, what baseball team do you want to support?" Each time the (person) struggles to answer and begins the mouth movements to get under way, the next question is asked. You ask a question, just start a pause, and don't give him a chance to respond. With the next question you wait, but not quite long enough. You're so earnest, and it frustrates them until finally they say, "Will you shut up? The answer is . . ."[8]

This technique, called "building expectancy" by Erickson, and "stacking" by Bandler and Grinder, is a powerful way to get reluctant people to open up to you. Its power comes from the need for completion in each of us.

This is a technique used quite extensively, and probably unintentionally, by Charlie Rose, the PBS talk show host. Rose, when he asks questions often stacks several of them, one on top of the other, frequently inserting an editorial comment in between. It's an amazingly baroque style that infuriates some people, but has the inevitable effect of building the response potential of the guest.

Another powerful tactic to get people to open up to you is giving permission to withhold, while simultaneously embedding suggestions to open up. Erickson describes his use of this approach:

> Sometimes in the first interview it is necessary to help someone talk. People come to tell you about their problems and yet are reluctant to discuss them. One way to deal with this is to say, "This is your first interview with me. You tell me you want to talk about some very painful things. In other words, I judge there are some things you'd rather not tell me. I think you ought not tell me those things you just can't endure

telling me. Tell me the things that you can, with the least amount of pain. Be sure you hold back the things you can't bear to tell me." The person starts to talk, and at the end of the hour will say, "Well, I've told you all the things I can't bear to tell you." What they do is select. They think, "Can I dare tell this or not? I'm free to withhold it, but I guess I can tell this one." They always vote in favor of telling. They postpone the telling, but that's what withholding is.[9]

If you examine this passage closely you'll find that Erickson embeds the suggestion "tell me" six times in six sentences that ostensibly give the client permission to withhold. The technique is unsurpassed in its subtle avoidance of creating resistance at the conscious level.

When confronted with a person who is unwilling to open up to you, you might find useful this variation of Erickson's phrasing: "I don't want you to tell me anything you don't want to tell me. Just tell me everything you feel comfortable telling me and everything I need to know to fully understand your situation."

If this sounds manipulative, consider the kinds of embedded suggestions people frequently and unwittingly give to loved ones:

Johnny, don't *put that in your mouth*!
Susie, don't you ever *speak to me that way*!
Sam, I don't know, this place is enough to *drive you crazy*!
Jill, don't run out into the street. You might *get hit by a car.*

To avoid such suggestions, state your wants and needs in the affirmative:

Johnny, *put that stick down* please.
Susie, I'd prefer you to *use a more pleasant tone* when you speak to me.
Sam, let's find a place where we can *calm down* and think.

Jill, *play in the yard* so you will *be safe from the traffic.*

The power of embedded suggestions is considerable. Use them wisely.

Creative Uses of Confusion

Sometimes during the course of a discussion, the person with whom you're talking may become confused. When this happens, it's useful to be aware of a phenomenon that Milton Erickson discovered during graduate school, and was later reminded of on a city street, in 1923:

> One windy day as I was on my way to attend the first formal seminar on hypnosis conducted in the United States a man came rushing around the corner of a building and bumped hard against me as I stood bracing myself against the wind. Before he could recover his poise to speak to me, I glanced elaborately at my watch and courteously, as if he had inquired the time of day, I stated, "It's exactly 10 minutes of two," though it was actually closer to 4:00 p.m. and I walked on. About a half a block away, I turned and saw him still looking at me, undoubtedly still puzzled and bewildered by my remark.[10].

As Erickson strolled on, he remembered other occasions when he had pulled similar stunts. Once he had thwarted the attempts of his college physics laboratory partner to do the portion of an experiment that both wanted to do. As they were dividing the equipment, Erickson, at the crucial moment, said quietly but with intensity, "That sparrow really flew to the right, then suddenly flew left, and then up and I just don't know what happened after that."

As his partner stared blankly at him, Erickson proceeded to gather up the equipment for the favored part of the experiment and got busily to work. Bewildered, his partner gathered up what Erickson had left him. Not until their work was almost finished did the partner notice that he was doing the part of the experiment he had planned to avoid.

Erickson later refined this technique by combining confusion with commands, both embedded and explicit, to produce a desired response. The operating principle here seems to be this: When a person is in a state of confusion, he or she will respond to the first clear directive that is given. It's a bit like a drowning man gasping for air: He will accept any air given him without stopping to question where it came from, or whether it "makes sense." People crave completion, wholeness.

Individuals trained in crowd control learn to use this confusion technique. In a riot, for example, a state of confusion often prevails until someone brings the situation under control by issuing clear, firm directions. By giving people in confusion a clear directive, you can guide them quite easily and with a minimum of resistance: "Remain calm. Get up and walk quietly to the exit."

Handling Objections

There are a number of ways to handle objections, depending on the nature of the objection and the personality of the person doing the objecting. Here are a few suggestions:

1. *Accept and use the objection.* Whenever a person objects to your idea, or to a part of it, keep in mind that there is energy behind the objection. With skill, you can use that energy and redirect it toward your objective. Suppose, for example, you

have just suggested a course of action to your client, Byron Biggs:

You: Well, Byron, what do you think of this idea?

Byron: I don't know. I'm going to have to think about it some more.

You: That's good, Byron. I'm glad you're going to give this careful consideration because this is an important decision you're about to make. Let's stop for a moment and review briefly the points we've agreed on that apply to your situation. As we're going through these points, if you have any questions, please stop me so that you can make the best possible decision.

By accepting Byron's objection and then redirecting his attention back to the issue at hand, especially the points of agreement, you are increasing the likelihood that you can get a favorable decision now. Notice, too, that you embedded certain suggestions that are designed to nudge Byron toward closure: "give this careful consideration . . . this is an important decision you're about to make . . . make the best possible decision."

The next step is to go through the major points in your presentation and observe or ask for Byron's response to each. For example, "Do you have any questions about that, Byron?" "Is it clear, or would you like to know more about that?" It's vitally important that you clear up Byron's doubts during this process. Otherwise, he will choose to resolve them without you, thereby increasing the probability that you'll both lose. After you've gone through this procedure, you'll be in a much better position to get the decision then and there, or at least to know what you have to do next.

2. *Agree with the feeling.* Sometimes it's virtually impossible to agree with certain ideas, or even a small part of certain ideas, without violating your own sense of integrity.

When such a situation arises, you can always align yourself with the other person's feelings. For example:

Ms. Chan: I just don't feel that your idea makes any sense for me now.

You: I can appreciate that feeling, Ms. Chan. I've felt that way at times myself, as have some of my clients. On further consideration, however, this is what many have found . . . (Give some examples of people who reconsidered, to their advantage.)

When a person tells you how he or she feels, it is very important to validate the feeling, whether you can agree with the idea expressed or not. One reason for doing this involves the way most of us are treated as children. Well-intentioned authority figures, such as parents, teachers, and coaches, were taught by other well-intentioned authority figures that the way you deal with a recalcitrant child is to feign anguish, look him or her sternly in the eye, and proclaim, "I honestly can't understand how you can feel that way! After all we've tried to do for you!"

A variation on this routine, when even sterner measures are called for, is "No child of mine could ever feel that way!" This technique ensures that the child grows up being confused and quite defensive about his or her feelings, especially when those feelings are not socially acceptable ones. And if you, in a well-intentioned effort to overcome an objection, should reply with "Byron, I just don't know how you can feel that way about this wonderful idea!" you may trigger an anchor that will release years of suppressed hostility and rage.

It's a better idea to validate the feeling, and kinder, too. You'll be regarded as an ally rather than an enemy.

3. *Tell a story.* This is one of the most effective ways to avoid generating resistance at the conscious level. Milton Erickson was especially adept in telling stories (using metaphor)

to deal with highly resistant clients. Jay Haley describes Erickson's technique:

> The analogical, or metaphoric, approach . . . is particularly effective with resistant subjects, since it is difficult to resist a suggestion one does not know consciously that he is receiving . . .
>
> As a typical example, if Erickson is dealing with a married couple who have a conflict over sexual relations and would rather not discuss it directly, he will approach the problem metaphorically. He will choose some aspect of their lives that is analogous to sexual relations and change that as a way of changing the sexual behavior.
>
> He might, for example, talk to them about having dinner together and draw them out on their preferences. He will discuss with them how the wife likes appetizers before dinner, while the husband prefers to dive right into the meat and potatoes. Or the wife might prefer a quiet and leisurely dinner, while the husband, who is quick and direct, just wants the meal over with.
>
> If the couple begin to connect what they are saying with sexual relations, Erickson will "drift rapidly" away to other topics, and then he will return to the analogy. He might end such a conversation with a directive that the couple arrange a pleasant dinner on a particular evening that is satisfactory to both of them. When successful, this approach shifts the couple from a more pleasant dinner to more pleasant sexual relations without their being aware that he has deliberately set this goal.[11]

Telling a story invites the other person to put him or herself in the story and allows his or her unconscious mind to make the necessary connections. This technique has been used by master persuaders for thousands of years. The parables told by Christ are notable examples.

4. *Express curiosity or interest.* Frequently, by expressing curiosity or interest, you can get the other person to elaborate on his or her objection, perhaps even to modify or withdraw it:

Cynthia: I don't think I can do that right now.

You: Really? That's interesting. I would have thought this would be the ideal time for you to do it. I'd be curious to know what prevents you from doing it now.

Cynthia: Well, I've got so many other things going on right now. I'd have to rearrange my schedule, and that would be a hassle.

Now you have something to work with. Perhaps you could offer to help Cynthia with some of her other priorities so that she could get to yours sooner. Whenever people tell you they don't have the time to do something that would be to their advantage, it probably means that they are not very good at managing their time. An offer to help them out could very well mean the acceptance of your idea in return for the assistance.

5. *Paraphrase the objection.* This tactic, like expressing interest or curiosity, often prompts people to elaborate or modify their objections.

Roy: I admit it would probably save us money in the long run, but we really can't fit it into the budget right now. The boss would have a fit.

You: Let me make sure I understand you correctly, Roy. You say that you agree this program is probably cost-effective, but that your boss would get mad because it hasn't been budgeted for, is that right?

Roy: Yeah, that's what I said. What I meant was that I'd have a hell of a time getting her to spend any more money until after the first of the year.

> You: It certainly sounds like we'd have to be real
>   persuasive. If we sat down and gave it some
>   more thought, do you think we could come up
>   with a proposal she'd listen to?
>
> Roy: Yeah, maybe.

Again you have something to work with. And if you agree to do
most of the work in completing the proposal, there's a good
chance you'll get Roy's support. Especially if it becomes his
idea, too.

6. *Ask what it would take to convince the other person.*
This question can profitably be asked in at least several places
during the discussion with the persons you seek to persuade. It's
a good question to ask before you prepare your presentation, for
instance. Often people will tell you exactly what you need to do
in order to convince them. The same question can also be asked
when you seem to have reached an impasse during the
presentation itself, when the person balks at the moment of
decision or when an objection is raised. It has the effect of
taking pressure off you while opening the discussion for new
information. The immediate goal is satisfied: Keep the
discussion moving until you see an opening.

7. *Confront with the brutal truth.* This is the last resort, for
people whom you think should act but are delaying without
apparent reason. It requires that you simply state the statistical
truth: namely, that a delay now means in all likelihood no action
ever on your proposal.

> Jane: Maybe you'd better call me back (this phrase is
>   being repeated now for the umpteenth time). I
>   don't have time to act on it now.
>
> You: I can appreciate your wanting to give this idea
>   careful consideration, but I can't understand
>   what has changed since the last several times

I've come by. May I be candid? In my experience, when people hesitate to act on an idea like this, they will never act on it, and will therefore never benefit from it. It's a sad fact that if I walk out the door now without a decision from you, the chances are less than one in ten that you'll ever benefit from this idea.

This statement should be uttered with the utmost gravity and sincerity, and then you should wait for a response. This becomes the put-up-or-shut-up moment. You want a decision. Even a negative response is better than the interminable process that can ensue when people repeatedly tell you to "call back later." Some people will keep this up indefinitely, wasting both your time and theirs. It makes better sense to have a final decision now, and be done with it one way or the other.

8. *Acknowledge and persist.* This has been tagged the "broken record" in assertiveness training and means just that: continuing to tell another person what you want in spite of all objections to the contrary. It would go something like this:

Lee: I just don't think I want to right now.
You: I realize you don't want to now, and I'd like very much for you to do it.
Lee: Nah, I just don't want to.
You: I understand that, and I'd like you to do it anyway.
Lee: Gee, I'd really rather wait 'til later.
You: I know you'd rather wait 'til later, and I'd like you to go ahead with it now.

This conversation may not be unfamiliar to parents of teenage sons and daughters whose lively eagerness does not always include homework. The idea here is to keep acknowledging (pacing) the other person's reluctance and pressing ahead (leading) in spite of it.

Very few people can withstand such persistence. Most will give in after no more than five attempts just to get us off their backs; seven is about the maximum number of times another person can resist such persistence. And although initially this technique may seem antithetical to the philosophy of flowing with resistance, notice that first you accept (pace) each rebuff, before stating your own position (lead). This approach works especially well with people who have to be prodded to get them to act. Admittedly, it's not a particularly enjoyable tactic to use on other people, but some individuals leave you little choice.

Dealing with Resistant Personality Types

As I mentioned earlier, it's a good idea to regard resistance in another person as something you've generated. At times, however, you may be forced to deal with people who seem always to be contrary, regardless of who they're relating to. Here are some suggestions for dealing with this type of individual:

1. *Play the devil's advocate.* Suppose you're presenting an idea to Mr. Snide, who starts objecting strongly to your proposal, perhaps even focusing part of the attack on you personally. There's a technique that you can use effectively in such a situation to take the heat off yourself. The technique is sometimes referred to as the "Hot Seat," and this is how it works. After your prospect has leveled a series of objections at you and your idea, get up out of your chair and walk thoughtfully over to him, sit down in a chair close to him (or stand in a neutral area near him), and then turn toward the empty chair. Say, "You know, Mr. Snide, if I were in your position" (which is exactly where you are now, physically), "I'd

probably be asking those same questions, and I'd want to have some good answers to them." You then restate his objections (slightly rephrasing the more personal ones in less vitriolic terms) while gesturing in the direction of the empty chair. You are now physically and by extension, psychologically on his side, playing the devil's advocate to your own proposition. This can defuse the attack and turn a potentially destructive adversarial relationship into a cooperative venture. Of course, after you play the devil's advocate in attacking your own proposition, you had better have good replies to his objections.

This technique can have a curious and profound effect on the other person, acting in some ways like the confusion technique mentioned earlier. It shifts the ground, so to speak, and can have the effect often referred to as "reverse psychology." With individuals who feel some inner need to disagree with anything anyone else says, the effect of your attacking your own proposition can often cause them to take the opposite point of view. This then places them in the rather interesting position of feeling a compulsion to defend your original idea.

2. *Suggest the opposite.* This technique resembles devil's advocate. But instead of telling the other person what you want, and then shifting the ground when your seat becomes too hot, you begin your presentation by suggesting the opposite of what you want the other person to do or to agree with. The rationale for this admittedly manipulative approach is that it's much easier to flow with: Get into alignment with the firmly established behavioral patterns of others, rather than to try to block or change them. For example, say you find yourself in the unenviable position of having to gain the support and cooperation of someone you know will typically "polarize" (to use one of Bandler and Grinder's favorite expressions). Instead of leveling with him or her, begin your discussion by suggesting the opposite, or implying that he probably can't do what you want him to. For example:

> You: I realize you probably don't have the authority to
>   OK this requisition, J.B., but I was wondering if
>   you could give me your advice on how to get it
>   done.
> J.B.:   What do you mean I don't have the authority!
>   Let me see that!

Or perhaps you want J.B. to have the office walls painted
yellow:

> You: You know, J.B., I just don't think this yellow is
>   right for the office. I know that several studies
>   have indicated that yellow is supposed to be a
>   good color for a working environment, but I
>   don't buy all that psychological mumbo-jumbo.
>   What do you think?

Of course, J.B. will be forced by some inner compulsion to
want to go with the yellow, and will probably throw in a five-
minute lecture on his interest in the psychological implications
of each color in the rainbow. You can listen politely and then
reluctantly agree that J. B. is probably right and that yellow
might not be such a bad color after all.

Manipulative? Of course it is, but not in a destructive way.
After all, you both win: you get what you want, which is yellow
walls, and J. B. gets what he wants, which is to do the opposite
of whatever you suggest. In this instance, manipulative means
"skillfully using the resources available to you," and one of the
major resources here is the behavior pattern presented by the
other person.

3. *Command and announce.* This delightful stratagem was
initially suggested by the late psychologist Lloyd Homme. It
proposes a way to control not only your own behavior but also
the behavior of others. At least it gives the appearance of

control, which for this purpose is close enough to the real thing. It works especially well with dictatorial types, who can make life stressful and miserable for those who have to work with them. Harriet has been trying to deal with Don, her boss, for the two years she's worked for him. She's been under a great deal of stress because Don never asks her to do anything; he orders her to do it, whether it be to get him a cup of coffee or to type an important letter. A typical interaction between Harriet and Don might go like this:

Don: (Sitting at his desk, busily shuffling papers. He doesn't even look up when Harriet enters.) Harriet, get me a cup of coffee, and find the file on the Danvers company, and after you've done that, finish the letter to Donegin. I want it by ten o'clock.

Harriet: (Fumes silently) Yes, of course. Will that be all?

Don: Yeah. (Harriet exits in a quiet rage, her stomach churning.)

Harriet feels like an unwilling puppet on a string. As long as she has worked for Don, she has done everything she can think of to get him to treat her like something more than a robot. She's even leveled with him and told him that she feels miserable when he orders her around without any apparent regard for her feelings. But nothing has worked so far, and she feels frustrated in her inability to improve the situation.

An alternative to this frustration lies in the "Command" technique. The rules are deceptively simple: Observe what the other person is doing or is about to do, and simply command him or her to do it, making it appear as if you are in control of the other person's behavior. This is a particularly effective tactic for dealing with dictatorial types such as Don.

A variation of "Command" is "Announcement," in which you announce what you are doing or are about to do, which puts you in control of your own behavior. When Harriet masters this move, an interaction with Don will go something like this:

Harriet: (Entering Don's office) Don, I'm going down the hall (announcement) and I'd like you to tell me if you want a cup of coffee (command).

Don: (Looking perplexed) Huh, sure, Harriet. Thanks. (Harriet exits and returns a few minutes later with Don's coffee.)

Harriet: Don, I'm going to finish the Donegin letter now (announcement). Here's your coffee. If it's not exactly the way you like it, I want you to tell me and I'll get you another cup (command).

Don: (Still confused) Um, sure, Harriet. Thanks.

If you examine this scene, you'll find that Harriet has put Don in a double bind. He can no longer easily order her around without at the same time obeying her orders. She has taken control of the situation, controlling her own behavior by announcing it and controlling his behavior by commanding him to act in precisely the way he's been accustomed to acting. And by commanding Don to be Don, Harriet has created his dilemma: If he tells her to do what she has just commanded him to do (get the coffee, take the coffee back, and so on) then he is in effect obeying her. If, on the other hand, he does not "obey" her by telling her what to do, then he is in effect doing what she really wants him to do, namely, relinquishing his authoritarian manner. In addition, whatever move Don makes (or doesn't make), he is responding to Harriet rather than she responding to him. Harriet has shifted the locus of control from Don to herself.

The dynamics of this relationship reflect a systems view of human interaction: Change one part of a system, and the other part(s) of the system will change in response, in order to reestablish a balance. Here the system is composed of two people, and because there is no way that Harriet can directly cause Don to change, she is left only with the option of changing herself.

And by changing her own behavior, she can depend on the fact that Don will change in response to her.

The secret is knowing what kind of change to make in your own behavior until you get a response in the other person that is acceptable to you. Having enough variety in your behavioral repertoire is very important here. Again, requisite variety is the key.

Note that in changing her behavior toward Don, Harriet has also shifted her attitude toward him. She has reframed the entire relationship, a subject we'll take up next.

The Gentle Art of Reframing

Throughout this book, we have stressed the importance of being able to share the other person's understanding and/or experience. Reframing another person's perception of a particular situation or state of affairs requires that you first be able to understand how the other person is perceiving the situation. You need to see it from the other person's point of view, to be able to ask yourself the same kinds of questions the other person is asking himself or herself, and to feel it the way the other person is feeling it. To reframe means just that: It means to *re*-frame the other person's perception, with the result that the other person sees the situation in a different way. To do this it's important that you be able to see through the other person's current frame. Reframing requires that you be able first to share his or her frame of reference.

Reframing requires only that we allow something new the chance to develop. In *The Dancing Wu Li Masters*, Gary Zukav's statement about the field of the "new physics" applies as well to all areas of life:

> I call something nonsense if it does not agree with the rational edifices that we carefully have constructed.

However, there is nothing intrinsically valuable about these edifices. In fact, they themselves often are replaced by more useful ones. When that happens, what was nonsensical from an old frame of reference can make sense from a new frame of reference, and the other way around.[12]

Perhaps the most popular instance of reframing is that of the glass of water that is half-full. Or is it half-empty? This, of course, depends entirely on your point of view. It depends on whether you're the optimist or the pessimist. Generally when you're optimistically presenting an idea to a resistant person, the roles are clearly defined. And so is the task you have before you, which is to reframe the other's perception, to enable him or her to see the situation from a different point of view. This now-classic ambiguous figure illustrates the problem:

Do you see the young woman or the old woman? They're both there, but one is probably more prominent than the other. In order to see the one you have to be able, at least momentarily, to not see the other. This state of affairs frequently describes the process that occurs when you encounter resistance from others. You may be looking at the same thing but seeing it from a different point of view.

If you're looking at the old woman and wish to see the young woman, you have to shift your point of view, up and slightly to the left. Look down and slightly to the right if you can see the young woman and would like to be able to see the old woman. Or see the mouth of the old woman as the choker of the young woman. See the left eye of the old woman as the left ear of the young woman. Or see the nose of the old woman as the outline of the cheek and jaw of the young woman. Or see the partially revealed right eyelash of the old woman as the eyelash of the young woman, and so on.

In other words, you must reframe your perception of the one to see the other. As Bandler and Grinder put it, "Reframing is a way of getting people to say 'Hey, how else can I do this?'"[13]

Most of the notable achievements of the human mind have involved reframing. Copernicus and Darwin have altered irrevocably the way we regard, respectively, the movement of the planets and the origin of species. Both of these achievements were accomplished in spite of stiff resistance (resistance that, in some quarters, continues to this day). Perhaps an even more startling reframing process is now underway in the natural and physical sciences, to cause us to look again at our notions of ourselves as individual human beings occupying a planet with other individual human beings. The new idea is that we are all one. The earth is like a single organism. All humanity is one humanity, and we share life with all things, including stones and stars. This is, of course, not a new idea. It was suggested in the sixth century BC by Heraclitus, and has been suggested by poets and philosophers since then. But ours is an age of science, and it is the scientist's voice that so many listen to because it paces the belief that from science not philosophy, not poetry, not religion will come the answers to our deepest questions.

How to Reframe

In the last section, Adrienne accepted Atherton's initial resistance to a new work flow procedure and then redirected his energy into a problem-solving mode. In the following example, observe how Adrienne reframes Griggs' concerns about a new computer system:

> Griggs: I just don't think we can afford it right now. For some time now, I've wanted a better system too, the best on the market, as a matter of fact. But the price just seems too high.

It's possible Griggs isn't sure that enough money is available in the budget at the present time to warrant the huge outlay that Adrienne's plan entails. She begins by pacing his concern. Then she leads by probing for deletions:

> Adrienne: Yes. It's an expensive system we're talking about. But I need some clarification. What do you mean by "the price seems to high"? Do you mean that we don't have enough in the budget for the initial outlay? Or do you mean that we can't be sure the system will be cost-effective over the next few years?

Adrienne determines that what Griggs really isn't sure of is not the initial outlay of funds, but rather the cost-effectiveness of the new computer system over an extended period of time. She proceeds:

> Adrienne: If I may, I'd like to back up for a moment. You've said before that you wanted a dependable system, one that can handle the department's tasks. I certainly feel the same way.

Adrienne has here adroitly taken some effective steps in dealing with resistance. First by gathering information, by asking not "Why?" but "What?" ("What do you mean by _____?"), she has filled in and clarified needed information. Having determined the real objection to the new system, she now has clearer lines of communication with the person she must convince. She found out specifically what her boss meant when he said, "The price just seems too high." Adrienne can now proceed to elaborate its cost-effectiveness and in the process gently reframe Griggs' perceptions of the new system.

The facts she has gathered are these: The initial outlay for the new computer system amounts to $8000, more than Griggs can justify in his budget. But the capacity of this advanced system will free department members to perform certain tasks being done at the rate of $20 per hour by part-time help. At the rate of ten such hours a week saved ($200 per week), savings over the first fiscal year alone would approximate $10400.

Thus, the actual cost of the system is considerably less and well within the department's budget. Griggs' thinking on the matter has been substantially reframed; suddenly, the old system's days are numbered.

Here's another humorous example of reframing, by Charles Shultz:

© Charles Shultz, 1980

As we see here, Snoopy has successfully reframed Charlie Brown's perception of just who should ride and who should pull. The intervening conversation between Charlie's proposal and Charlie's pulling may have gone something like this:

Snoopy: Charlie, your idea sounds like great fun, but I think we ought to discuss a point or two. As I understand it, you're suggesting that we take your skateboard, put one of us on it while the other pulls. (Snoopy establishes an area of agreement.)

Charlie: Right. Right. You pull and I ride. That other kid and his dog were really moving.

Snoopy: Charlie, tell me something. How much do you weigh?
           (Snoopy is at the information-gathering stage.)

Charlie: Um, about eighty-eight pounds.

Snoopy: Gosh. I didn't realize you were that big. (As Charlie begins beaming, Snoopy lightly places his paw on Charlie's forearm and exerts slight pressure, thus anchoring Charlie's response.) You know, that's eighty-three pounds more than I weigh. In fact, if I pull you, I'll have to lug about twenty times my own body weight, wheels or no wheels. That doesn't seem to me as if we would be moving with "blinding speed."

Charlie: (Mulling things over) Um, Snoopy, that's not exactly what I had in mind.

Snoopy: (Seeming not to notice what it is that Charlie does have in mind) On the other hand, if you were to pull me I barely weigh five pounds ringing wet. Why, you'd hardly feel the drag. We'd both be flying in no time. I think it's just plain logic, Charlie. (As Snoopy emphasizes Charlie's name, he simultaneously triggers the previously established anchor by again raising his paw, putting it on Charlie's forearm and applying light pressure.) I'm convinced that you'll do a much better job of pulling than I could. (Snoopy hops aboard, leaving Charlie a bit bewildered.) He may not have the eloquence of a Mark Antony reframing the perceptions of his roman countrymen, but Snoopy distinguishes himself by getting the job done. And that's what it's all about.

Disarming Verbal Anger and Hostility

Whenever someone attacks you, your idea, or something with which you're associated, the first issue to deal with is not the content of the attack but rather the attacker's anger or hostility. A mistake people often make when attacked is to try to defend themselves, their idea, or their association. In most instances, defensiveness is a tactical error, because it can easily be taken by the other person as a counterattack and as such serves only to increase the level of anger or hostility, as in the following exchange:

    Attacker: You really fouled up this time!
    Defender: I did not!
    Attacker: You did too!!
    Defender: Did not!!
    Attacker: Did too!!!
    Defender: Did not!!!
    Attacker: Did too!!!

A much better response is to pace and then lead, aligning with the attacker's momentum, as follows:

    Attacker: You really fouled up this time!
    You: You may be right. What did I do this time?

| Attacker: | You said you were going to deliver my widgets by Thursday and here it is Friday and no widgets. |
| You: | In that case, I can understand why you're angry. Let's find out what we can do about this to get you your widgets and make sure this doesn't ever happen again. |

The first step in dealing with a verbal attack is to defuse the attacker, align with his or her energy, and then redirect it, just as you would deal with any other form of resistance. There are at least two ways of doing this: (1) agree with the content, and (2) agree with or validate the feeling.

In the example just given, you agreed with the content by saying, "You may be right." The reason for doing this is that you avoid threatening the attacker, who may already be so emotionally out of control that anything you say might be construed as a counterattack and would serve only to escalate his or her own attack. Avoid adding fuel to the fire.

This does not mean that you acquiesce to the attacker. Agreement (or alignment) and acquiescence are at opposite ends of the continuum. Agreement is active, whereas acquiescence is passive. Acquiescence is simply capitulation, and is not effective in producing the desired outcome, which is to lead the other person to a constructive discussion.

The statement, "You may be right," has truly magical power when uttered sincerely, without rancor, sarcasm, or defensiveness. It gives the impression of agreement while in fact leaving open an infinite number of possibilities. (For example, it also implies "You may be wrong," or "Maybe there's another way of looking at the situation.") But psychologically it defuses the energy behind the attack and enables you to redirect that energy into a problem-solving mode and toward a solution of the attacker's problem.

If you think that what the attacker is saying is probably a valid criticism, you might say, "You're probably right." If you're certain the criticism or attack is justified, then "You are right" might be the most appropriate response. Whatever your choice of phrasing, keep in mind that the first issue to deal with is the anger, the hostility, not the content of the attack. Deal with the content after you've disarmed the assailant. But what if the attacker is especially vehement, not allowing you to say anything but charging at you with a verbal barrage? A useful and effective strategy is to let him or her release some of the energy while you absorb it quietly and unemotionally. Then, when the attacker has cooled down, get into agreement and redirect. This simple strategy can change what might otherwise be a disastrous encounter into a mutually productive one.

If you cannot sincerely agree with anything the attacker is saying, or cannot bring yourself to admit even the possibility that his or her criticism might be justified, then get into alignment with the feeling. No matter what the other person is feeling, you will always be theoretically correct when you say, "If I were in your position, I'm sure I'd feel the same way you do." The rationale behind this is simple: If you had the other person's genetic and personal history, it is inevitable you'd feel exactly the same way he or she does at the present moment. Another way of saying this is that if you *were* the other person you would be feeling the same way he or she is feeling right now. This may sound like a verbal trick, a semantic device, but this verbal trick could well save your job, your relationship, or even your life some day.

162 The Magic of Rapport

Summary

In this final part of the book, we've examined what resistance is and what you can do about it. Perhaps the most important thing you can do initially is to regard resistance as something over which you have control. You can alter the other person's resistance by getting into agreement or alignment with it, instead of trying to fight it. It's much easier to move from agreement to agreement than from disagreement to agreement.

Resistance to change is prompted by uncertainty and the fear of interrupted social relationships. Resistance to change can be most effectively dealt with by reducing the uncertainty and by involving those most affected by the change in both analyzing the problem and implementing the solution.

Life is not a contest. It's possible to relate to people in such a manner that everyone is a winner, rather than some winners and some losers.

Encouraging reluctant people to open up can be achieved by the tactic of initially frustrating their answers to questions. Also, you can embed suggestions in conversations with such people.

Creative uses of confusion involve using the other person's bewilderment to suggest directions and outcomes. Creativity can be used to turn confusion into an opportunity to overcome resistance.

Resistant personality types are best dealt with by reframing, subtly shifting the context of the resistance so that the resistance itself disappears. This is best accomplished by first finding an area of agreement with the other person. Another especially effective technique is Command and Announcement.

Suggestions for Practice

1. When you encounter resistance in your dealings with others, look for something in what they have said or done that you can agree with before bringing out the area(s) of disagreement. For example: "I agree with what you just said about (area of agreement). I'm having some difficulty with (area of disagreement), though. Can you help me understand your position better?"

2. When someone resists you, become aware of how this makes you feel. Be especially aware of your own defensiveness, which often manifests as a tightness in your chest accompanied by an inability to pay attention to what the other person is saying or doing. Notice whether at this moment it is easy or difficult for you to find something to agree or align with in what the other person is saying or feeling.

3. Have fun with other people's resistance. Keep your sense of humor and remember that if you were in their position (that is, had their parents and their personal history) you would probably be reacting exactly as they are in the present situation.

Part Four
Notes

[1] The point here is that people want to be right and will do almost anything to sustain the belief that they are right. Wars continue to be waged around this central issue. It's therefore a wiser, and safer, tactic to validate a particular part of another person's belief, at least initially, moving from an area of agreement (pacing) to areas of potential disagreement or misunderstanding (leading). It's much easier to move from agreement to agreement than from disagreement to agreement.

[2] Paul R. Lawrence, "How to Deal with Resistance to Change," *Harvard Business Review,* 1969, 47 (1) p. 4.

[3] Lawrence, p. 166.

[4] Lawrence, p. 168.

[5] Lester C. Thurow, *The Zero-Sum Society* (New York: Basic Books,1980), p. 23.

[6] R.G.H. Sui, *The Craft of Power* (New York: Wiley, 1979), p. 148.

[7] Wallace Stevens, *Poems* (New York: Alfred A. Knopf), pp. 61-63.

[8] Jay Haley, *Uncommon Therapy: The Psychiatric Techniques of Milton H. Erickson, M.D.* (New York: Norton, 1973), p. 245.

[9] Milton H. Erickson, *Advanced Techniques of Hypnosis and Therapy: Selected Papers of Milton H. Erickson, M.D.,* ed. Jay Haley (New York: Grune & Stratton, 1967), p. 131.

[10] Erickson, p. 131.

[11] Haley, pp. 2728.

[12] Gary Zukav, *The Dancing Wu Li Masters* (New York: Morrow, 1979), p. 187.

[13] Richard Bandler and John Grinder, *Frogs Into Princes* (Moab, Utah: Real People press, 1969), p. 183.

A Final Word

In *The Magic of Rapport*, I have attempted to present as simply and clearly as I can some of the most effective approaches I know for establishing rapport and getting the support and cooperation of the people you live and work with. At times I've oversimplified for the sake of clarity and applicability. *The Magic of Rapport* offers a model, an approach to effective communication. A model is just that—a model. A model is not "reality." A model is a way of saying, "Here's a way of looking at something so that it will make sense and be of value." But as Alfred Korzybski, the founder of General Semantics, once said, "The map is not the territory." The model is not the reality. Pacing is doing something similar to another person; leading is doing something different. To establish rapport with the other person you pace; to influence the other person you lead. Whenever you're with another person, you're either pacing or leading.

You can pace all observable behavior. You can also pace another person's internal experience, such as perceptual modes and decision strategies. Pacing resistance enables you to align yourself with the other person's energy or momentum and then redirect it.

Underlying this model is a systems approach to human interaction. Systems are dynamic; when you change one part of the system, you can predict that other parts of the system will change in response, to re-establish equilibrium. The pace/lead model seems to work because when two people are in synchrony, they form a balanced system. If one person changes his or her behavior (leads), then the other person is likely to change in response. (When you're in step with another person, the next step you take the other person is apt to follow.)

One of the problems that some people have with the notion of pacing is that they're afraid they might give up something of themselves, as if "personality" were somehow a scarce commodity that can be lost if you give it up momentarily to pace another person. There is very little danger of losing anything by pacing another person. As a matter of fact, quite the opposite is true. By pacing the other person, you are in a sense extending the range of "selves" you have—you are becoming more fully human, not less so. Pacing is a way of making peace with other people by making it possible for you to share a common experience or common understanding. This, after all, is what communication is about, sharing something in common with other people.

A major objective of this book has been to offer some practical suggestions that will enable you to work and live more productively and harmoniously with other people. Although most of the techniques and strategies suggested here are simple to understand and to apply, that does not mean necessarily that they are easy. They take practice. In some cases, you may find that you're working against the pressure of old habits, some of which have been firmly in place since you were a small child. But with awareness and practice you should be able to create new patterns, ones that serve you rather than ones to which you are subservient.

Take one thing at a time and work on it for a few minutes each day until you find that you're doing it without thinking about it. For example, spend a few minutes each day synchronizing your rate of movement with that of a person or persons you're interacting with. One of the first things you'll probably notice is how different some people are. You might find yourself becoming slightly uncomfortable when you're pacing behavior that is outside your own comfort zone. Regard this as a good sign: It means that you are beginning to extend the range of possibilities for yourself. It's a bit like exercising muscles that haven't been used. Initially there is discomfort, but with exercise and use, you become comfortable with the new behavior and incorporate it into your repertoire. In a sense with each new behavior, you have a new self to add to the many selves you already possess.

We now have adequate tools for the destruction of our entire planet. It is imperative that we develop and refine the tools available for mutual cooperation and support. We know what works. The task now is to apply it.

Throughout this book we've discussed techniques and strategies for getting what you want through and with other people. But underlying the discussion is really something else. It's about an attitude, an approach, a philosophy, with which to encounter other people.

Technique alone is not enough. The Germans have a word—*Dasein*—which is difficult to translate into an exact English equivalent. It's usually rendered as "ground of being," after which the discussion tends to become quite heady, esoteric to the point of being almost incomprehensible. But it's an important concept. In the context of this material, it has to do with your attitude, your intentions, when you encounter others.

Your ground of being when you're with another person critically determines how that other person is going to respond to you. If your attitude, your intention, is to do everything you can to produce an outcome that is in the best interests both of yourself and of the other person you will communicate it.

If in addition you can truly enter into the other person's reality, to stand together upon the same ground of being, to share the same Dasein, it's likely that both of you will be able to produce an outcome, a result, that is mutually rewarding and satisfying.

In his intriguing little book, *The Lazy Man's Guide to Enlightenment*, Thaddeus Golas defines love in an interesting way. "Love," he says, "is the action of being in the same space with other beings." The operative word here is action. In this context, in the confines of *The Magic of Rapport*, what is called pacing is an act of love. It is the action of being in the same space with another person. It is an entering into another person's reality to share it with him or with her. It is being on common ground. It is an act of communication, which is a communion, which is a sharing of the same understanding or experience. It is also a position of power, because it is a place where you are not alone. It is a place where you and the other person join energies and move together toward a common goal. It is a place where you have rapport. And where there is rapport there is magic, and where there is magic there is power. Use it wisely.

A Selected Bibliography

Alessandra, Anthony J., Ph.D., and Phillip S. Wexler, with Jerry D. Deen. 1979. *Non-Manipulative Selling*. Reston, VA: Reston Publishing Company, Inc.

Andreas, Connirae, Ph.D., and Steve Andreas, M.A. 1989. *Heart of the Mind: Engaging Your Inner Power to Change with Neuro-Linguistic Programming*. Moab, Utah: Real People Press.

Ashby, W. Ross. 1956. *An Introduction to Cybernetics*. New York: Methuen.

Bacharach, Samuel B., and Edward J. Lawler. 1980. *Power and Politics in Organizations*. San Francisco: Jossey-Bass, Inc.

Bagley, Dan S. III, and Edward J Reese. 1988. *Beyond Selling: How to Maximize Your Effectiveness*. Capitola, CA: Meta Publications.

Bandler, Richard, and John Grinder. 1979. *Frogs into Princes: Neurolinguistic Programming*. Moab, Utah: Real People Press.

Blanchard, Kenneth, Ph.D., and Spencer Johnson, M.D. 1982. *The One Minute Manager*. New York: William Morrow.

Bramson, Robert M., Ph.D. 1981. *Coping With Difficult People*. Garden City, NY: Anchor Press/Doubleday.

Brown, J. A. C. 1963. *Techniques of Persuasion: From Propaganda to Brainwashing*. Great Britain: Penguin Books, Ltd.

Burley-Allen, Madelyn. 1982. *Listening: The Forgotten Skill*. New York: John Wiley & Sons, Inc.

Carnegie, Dale. 1936. *How To Win Friends And Influence People*. New York: Simon & Schuster.

Cuming, Pamela. 1981. *The Power Handbook: A Strategic Guide to Organizational and Personal Effectiveness.* Boston: CBI Publishing Co., Inc.

Davis, Martha, Ph.D. 1982. *Interaction Rhythms: Periodicity in Communicative Behavior.* New York: Human Sciences Press.

Dilts, Robert. 1994. *Strategies of Genius: Volume II.* Capitola, CA: Meta Publications.

Dilts, Robert. 1998. *Modeling With NLP.* Capitola, CA: Meta Publications.

Eakins, Barbara, and R. Gene Eakins. 1978. *Sex Differences in Human Communication.* Boston: Houghton Mifflin Co.

Ekman, Paul, and Wallace V. Friesen. 1975. *Unmasking the Face.* Englewood Cliffs, NJ: Prentice-Hall, Inc.

Fisher, Roger, and William Ury. 1981. *Getting to Yes: Negotiating Agreement Without Giving In.* Boston: Houghton Mifflin Co.

Goleman, Daniel. 1979. "People Who Read People," in *Psychology Today*, July 1979/Vol. 13, No. 2, pp. 66-78.

Goleman, Daniel. 1995. *Emotional Intelligence.* New York: Bantam Books.

Goleman, Daniel. 1998. *Working with Emotional Intelligence.* New York: Bantam.

Haley, Jay, ed. 1973. *Uncommon Therapy: The Psychiatric Techniques of Milton H. Erickson, M.D.* New York: W. W. Norton & Co.

Haley, Jay. 1986. *The Power Tactics of Jesus Christ and Other Essays, 2nd Edition.* Rockville, MD: The Triangle Press.

Hall, Edward T. 1959. *The Silent Language.* Greenwich, CT: Fawcett Publications, Inc.

Harper, Robert G., Arthur N. Wiens, Joseph D. Matarazzo. 1978. *Nonverbal Communication: The State of the Art.* New York: John Wiley & Sons.

Hersey, Dr. Paul. 1984. *The Situational Leader.* New York: Warner Books.

Klein, Gary. 1999. *Sources of Power: How People Make Decisions*. Cambridge, MA: The MIT Press.

Kleinke, Chris L. 1975. *First Impressions: The Psychology of Encountering Others*. Englewood Cliffs, NJ: Prentice-Hall.

Kotter, John P. 1979. *Power in Management: How to Understand, Acquire, and Use It*. New York: Amacom.

Marshall, Lisa J. and Lucy D. Freedman. 1995. *Smart Work: The Syntax Guide for Mutual Understanding in the Workplace*. Dubuque, IA: Kendall/Hunt Publishing Company.

Mehrabian, Albert. 1971. *Silent Messages*. Belmont, CA: Wadsworth Publishing Co., Inc.

Mehrabian, Albert. 1972. *Nonverbal Communication*. Chicago: Aldine Publishing Co.

O'Connor, Joseph and John Seymour. 1990. *Introducing Neuro-Linguistic Programming*. London: Mandala.

Osborne, Cecil G. 1980. *The Art of Getting Along With People*. Grand Rapids, MI: Zondervan Publishing.

Peters, Thomas J. 1987. *Thriving on Chaos: Handbook for a Management Revolution*. New York: Knopf.

Rackham, Neil. 1988. *Spin Selling*. New York: McGraw-Hill.

Rogers, Carl, and F. J. Roethlisberger. 1979. "Barriers and Gateways to Communication," in *Harvard Business Review: On Human Relations*. New York: Harper and Row.

Ross, Raymond S., Ph.D., and Mark G. Ross, Ph.D. 1981. *Understanding Persuasion*. Englewood Cliffs, NJ: Prentice-Hall, Inc.

Satir, Virginia. 1972. *Peoplemaking*. Palo Alto, CA: Science and Behavior Books, Inc.

Seligman, Martin E.P. 1991. *Learned Optimism*. New York: Alfred A. Knopf.

Sheldon, William H., with the collaboration of C. Wesley Dupertuis and Eugene McDermott. *Atlas of Men: A Guide for Somatotyping the Adult Male at All Ages* (New York : Gramercy, c1954).

Sommer, Robert. 1978. *The Mind's Eye: Imagery in Everyday Life*. New York: Delta.

Tavris, Carol. 1982. *Anger: The Misunderstood Emotion*. New York: Simon and Schuster.

Thurow, Lester C., 1980. *The Zero-Sum Society*. New York: Basic Books.

Watzlawick, Paul, Ph.D. 1974. *Change: Principles of Problem Formation and Problem Resolution*. New York: W. W. Norton & Co., Inc.

Index